MARYLAND'S HISTORIC RESTAURANTS

and their recipes

JOHN F. BLAIR, *Publisher*
Winston-Salem, North Carolina

MARYLAND'S HISTORIC RESTAURANTS

and their recipes

by DAWN O'BRIEN
and REBECCA SCHENCK

Drawings by Bob Anderson

Library of Congress Cataloging in Publication Data

O'Brien, Dawn.
Maryland's historic restaurants and their recipes.

Includes index.
1. Cookery, American. 2. Cookery—Maryland. 3. Restaurants,
lunch rooms, etc.—Maryland. 4. Historic buildings—Maryland.
I. Schenck, Rebecca. II. Title.
TX715.0'284   1985   641.5'09752   85-15108
ISBN 0-89587-048-7

DEDICATION

For my two sisters, Jessica Roubaud and Marian Daugherty, who keep asking, "When are you going to dedicate a book to me?" This is it, girls!

Dawn O'Brien

For the families represented by these restaurants and for my own family—especially Gordon.

Rebecca Schenck

ACKNOWLEDGMENTS

Books like this don't just happen. A lot of people get in on the act. Researching the research comes first—that is, contacting the many agencies and societies within a state to find out where to go and what to look for. We are thankful to those who pointed us in the right direction and to many others who paved the roads for us in a variety of ways.

To: J. Charles Lehmann, Assistant Director of the Maryland Department of Economic and Community Development, who opened the paths for us to follow.

To: The Maryland chambers of commerce, tourism councils and public libraries, and in particular to Betty C. Callahan, Kay Morrow, Betty S. Stilt, Norma Grovermann, Jo Beynon, Cindy Kutchman and Richard Parsons, who did extra paving.

To: Doug Zima, who scouted out restaurants that we would not otherwise have found.

To: The chefs, who generously shared their time, talent and secrets with us.

To: The restaurateurs, who often did as much digging as we did in tracing stories.

To: The artist, Bob Anderson, who did such a splendid job with his pen and ink renderings of the restaurants of South Carolina that we talked him into doing the same for Maryland.

To: The editor, Ginny Hege, who edited with sensitivity, skill and kindness.

To: Daintry O'Brien, who helped with the driving, photography and testing of recipes.

To: Gordon Schenck for our beautiful cover shots as well as his help with testing and tasting.

To: All our guinea pigs (old and new to the series) who continue to flatter our efforts.

FOREWORD

"**A** good cook is a sorceress who dispenses happiness," said designer Elsa Schiaparelli. In the early days of my marriage, my cooking produced happiness—that is, if you equate giggles with happiness. In fact, my husband, John, still laughs about our first Thanksgiving. Having bought a "stuffed turkey" in the supermarket, I thought, "Oh good, I won't have to make stuffing." Yes indeed, old dummy actually cooked that bird with its own innards! Was it terrible? No, the turkey was quite moist and tasty. But that was four cookbooks ago, before I realized that creativity in the kitchen is often what your imagination can salvage from disaster.

You see, I am basically a lazy writer who is hooked on history. I say lazy because I prefer to do research in epicurean restaurants rather than in stuffy libraries. Especially when half of the research consists of delighting my tastebuds with the creativity of the world's finest chefs. Yeah, I know: "It's a tough job but somebody has to do it." What makes this work intriguing is that each state, in fact, each restaurant, is so different. But after eating myself through North Carolina's and Virginia's historic restaurants, I realized that the limitation of time necessitated collaborators for the series. Hence, I began looking for other lazy, or shall we say, sensually indulgent writers who are also into the *joie de vivre*.

For this book, co-author Rebecca Schenck, along with her architectural photographer husband, Gordon, and I have enjoyed Maryland's contrasts in fine food. From regional dishes enhanced with western Maryland maple syrup to endless variations on seafood cookery, we have found Maryland abundant in her culinary selection. Gordon, who uncomplainingly vows that he has tasted Maryland crab prepared in every possible way, is convinced that this crab is the tenderest that has ever crossed his palate, particularly the Crab Imperial at The Inn at Perry Cabin. My daughter Heather, on the other hand, votes for the dynamite desserts, especially the Cozy Restaurant's Blueberry Cassis Pie.

My daughter Daintry was surprised that a novice cook like herself could actually duplicate such masterpieces as the Penwick House's Mushroom Turnover. From the beginning that was one of my goals: to put unusually delicious recipes in a form that could easily be followed at home. It is creativity, not fancy cooking-school technique, that makes an ordinary cook into an extraordinary cook. The recipes included here may seem simple, but the creative touches of the chefs guarantee delicious results.

In collecting these recipes, Rebecca and I have been tutored by chefs who have studied at the famous cooking schools of the world. But these chefs are quick to point out that education was only one important ingredient in their success. Talent lies in starting with the basics and creating one's own thing.

Rebecca and I have tried to follow that course in this book. Our "basics" begin with restaurants housed in buildings that are over fifty years old. At that age or older, a structure generally has a good story to tell. In visiting these restaurants, we "do our own thing." We try to find the most intriguing story that the establishment has to offer and then weave that story in with our impressions of the food, décor and ambience. After sampling the restaurant's most popular offerings, we select several recipes, which are taken home to test. People often ask, "Why do you test every recipe if you've already eaten it at the restaurant?" The reason is simple: we must make sure that ingredients are correctly proportioned for home use and that the recipe is easy to follow.

We found that many of Maryland's historic restaurants have been in the same family for generations. We've met parents and children working together in the restaurants that were inherited from past generations. Rebecca confides that she expected the best part would be hearing and writing the stories, but now she feels that the best part has come from meeting the people who tell them. In these times of family polarity, we can't think of a nicer way to remember a state than to associate it with warm, family-accented stories. When we return home, we come not only with a new batch of recipes, but a new batch of people who have touched our lives in a special way.

CONTENTS

Foreword   *ix*

COMMANDER HOTEL   1
Ocean City

KATE BUNTING'S SEAFOOD HOUSE   5
Ocean City

CAPTAIN'S GALLEY   9
Crisfield

HOTEL INN RESTAURANT AND LOUNGE   13
Princess Anne

THE CHAMBERS   17
Easton

ROBERT MORRIS INN   21
Oxford

THE PASADENA   25
Royal Oak

THE INN AT PERRY CABIN   29
St. Michaels

HARRISON'S CHESAPEAKE HOUSE   33
Tilghman Island

KITTY KNIGHT HOUSE   37
Georgetown

FRAN O'BRIEN'S   41
Annapolis

HARRY BROWNE'S   45
Annapolis

McGARVEY'S SALOON & OYSTER BAR   49
Annapolis

MIDDLETON TAVERN   53
Annapolis

RIORDAN'S SALOON   57
Annapolis

THE TREATY OF PARIS RESTAURANT   61
Annapolis

THE PENWICK HOUSE   65
Dunkirk

BLAIR MANSION INN   69
Silver Spring

MRS. K'S TOLL HOUSE   73
Silver Spring

BROOK FARM INN OF MAGIC   77
Chevy Chase

NORMANDIE FARM   81
Potomac

OLD ANGLER'S INN   85
Potomac

BRASS ELEPHANT   89
Baltimore

CHESAPEAKE RESTAURANT   93
Baltimore

HAUSSNER'S RESTAURANT, INC.   97
Baltimore

SABATINO'S   101
Baltimore

SOCIETY HILL BAR, RESTAURANT AND HOTEL   105
Baltimore

COUNTRY FARE INN   109
Owings Mills

FIORI   113
Reisterstown

MILTON INN   117
Sparks

MANOR TAVERN   121
Monkton

COCKEY'S TAVERN   125
Westminster

MAGGIE'S   129
Westminster

MEALEY'S   133
New Market

BUSHWALLER'S   137
Frederick

MANAYUNK TAVERN   141
Frederick

THE PROVINCE   145
Frederick

COZY RESTAURANT   149
Thurmont

THE OTT HOUSE PUB AND RESTAURANT   153
Emmitsburg

OLD SOUTH MOUNTAIN INN   157
Boonsboro

DUTCH KITCHEN   161
Hagerstown

BISTRO   165
Cumberland

L'OSTERIA   169
Cumberland

FRED WARNER'S GERMAN RESTAURANT   173
Cresaptown

AU PETIT PARIS   177
Frostburg

THE CASSELMAN   181
Grantsville

PENN ALPS RESTAURANT   185
Grantsville

CORNISH MANOR   189
    Oakland

PC'S 1897 SALOON & EATERY   193
    Oakland

THE CHIMNEY CORNER   197
    Red House

Index   201

Captain John Smith, upon his exploration of the Chesapeake Bay, described Maryland as a "pleasant and delightsome land." His comment came in part from the abundance of fish, crabs, clams and oysters he found in the bay.

More than 370 years later, Marylanders still treat crabs, oysters and fish with reverence. You have my personal guarantee of finding in Maryland the best crab cakes you will ever eat. This book has the recipe. It is hard to beat fresh bay oysters on the half shell, but there are many other recipes here that will tempt you.

Leaving the Bay to travel upland, Maryland's food is influenced by a combination of Pennsylvania Dutch recipes and Virginia's Southern recipes. At one meal you can enjoy Crab Bisque, Sauerbraten and Southern Spoonbread. Top it off with some Apple Strudel from the orchard outside your restaurant window.

Baltimore, while known for steamed crabs and beer, is as continental as any European city. Just find the taste that suits you after a day at Harborplace.

Take your time and travel across Maryland from the Atlantic Ocean to the mountains. Slow down and sample the foods of the famous and not-so-famous restaurants and country inns mentioned here. Take this book along and have the chefs autograph it for you. They're as proud of their food as we are of our state.

Harry Hughes
Governor of Maryland

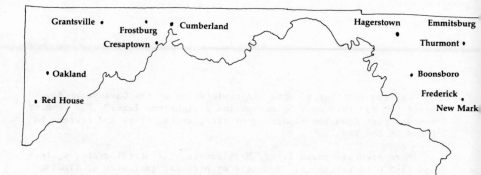

Grantsville •   •   • Cumberland   Hagerstown   Emmitsburg

Frostburg   • Thurmont •

Cresaptown •

• Oakland   • Boonsboro

• Red House   Frederick •

New Mark

Poto

Westminster

Monkton
Sparks

Reisterstown
Owings Mills

Baltimore

Georgetown

lver Spring
evy Chase

Annapolis

Dunkirk

St. Michaels
Easton
Tilghman Island
Royal Oak
Oxford

Ocean City

Princess Anne

Crisfield

COMMANDER HOTEL
Ocean City

COMMANDER HOTEL

"You'll never make a go of it—it's too far out of town," John Lynch was told when he built the Commander Hotel in 1930. It was on the ocean at 14th Street, and the Boardwalk ended at 15th. Now a strip of highrise hotels and resort condominiums extends another hundred blocks, and John Lynch, Jr., accepts reservations two to three years in advance.

Ocean City used to be a part of Assateague Island, the "place across," as Indians called the beautiful reef between the Atlantic and the mainland of Maryland and Virginia. The island embodies the mystery of shipwrecks, pirates and wild ponies, and for centuries its shoreline has been determined by wind and ocean. In 1933 a hurricane cut a channel at Ocean City and caused people to remember that "it is an ill wind turns none to good." The Ocean City Inlet is considered a major factor in the growth of the seaside resort. During some months of the year, Ocean City is now the second most populated city in Maryland.

Good information came from Tom, the maître d' in service at Commander Hotel for almost forty years. He talked while I ate in an L-shaped dining room whose bentwood chairs had slipcovered backs to match the draperies at shuttered windows. Walls in the room are "pulled" stucco—no paint—with a whiter lime on the ceiling. I could see why the room was selected to be in a motion picture.

The relaxing décor, with its just-right touches of cheerful pink and green, will make you want to linger over coffee and another Coconut Muffin at breakfast (Spoonbread on Friday mornings that would satisfy even your Aunt Mary) or a Rum Bun after dinner—all baked in Commander's kitchen.

People return to Commander Hotel year after year for family vacations or business conventions, knowing they can expect good food and comfort. The Knights of Columbus have come for thirty years. When I arrived—along with two hundred and fifty "St. John's Oldtimers"—the Maryland Soft Drink Bottlers had just left. There was hubbub in the lobby, and I picked up a sheet at the desk announcing an Irish

2

Wake Story Contest for the Oldtimers, to be judged by the oldest ones among them. I asked for an example of a story. The contest originator didn't want to give away the best, but he offered this: "Did you know Frank?" "No, but he's got a lovely set of teeth."

Poor Frank, if he didn't get to sink them into the Peach Brandy Pound Cake. John Lynch, Jr.'s family has this "melt-in-your-mouth" cake at home every Christmas, and the cake is also a regular offering on the menu for the Commander Boardwalk Cabaret that operates at Commander Hotel five nights a week during July and August. I hope to make a reservation soon.

I have a day all planned. I'll lie on the beach until I've had enough sun. Then I'll browse in shops along the Boardwalk, already knowing the way to Newmyer's in Commander's basement for a waffle cone or peanut brittle. After a nap, I'll enjoy the player piano in the Skipjack Lounge until the pianist comes to the baby grand. A glass of Mateus rosé will prepare me for dinner.

Commander Hotel is located on the ocean at 14th Street in Ocean City. Breakfast is served from 8:00 a.m. until 10:00 a.m., and dinner is served from 6:00 p.m. until 8:00 p.m., daily, mid-April until mid-October. Reservations are not necessary, but the phone number is (301) 289-6166.

COMMANDER HOTEL'S CAPTAIN JACK'S CARROT SALAD

6 cups canned, sliced carrots
1 green pepper, chopped
1 small onion, chopped
1 10-ounce can tomato soup
3/4 cup sugar
1 teaspoon prepared
  mustard

1 teaspoon Worcestershire
  sauce
3/4 cup cider vinegar
1 teaspoon salt
4 tablespoons salad oil
1 teaspoon black pepper

Mix all ingredients and chill overnight. Keeps well in refrigerator in a 3-quart covered casserole. Serves 12.

3

COMMANDER HOTEL'S SOUTHERN SPOONBREAD

1 pint milk
1 teaspoon salt
2/3 cup water-ground white
  cornmeal

1 tablespoon sugar
2 tablespoons margarine
3 eggs
2 teaspoons baking powder

In a large saucepan, heat milk, salt, cornmeal, sugar and margarine, stirring to prevent lumping, until the mixture is the consistency of stiff mush. Remove from heat and stir until mixture cools. Break eggs, one at a time, into mixture and stir hard after each addition. Add baking powder. Pour into a greased 3-quart baking dish or any pan that fills with batter to a depth of about 4 inches. Bake at 375 degrees for 30 to 40 minutes. Serves 8 to 10.

Note: Finished product should be moist, *not* dry like cornbread. It is traditionally served with a spoon. Do not use a shallow pan, or spoonbread will be too dry.

COMMANDER HOTEL'S PEACH BRANDY POUND CAKE

1 cup butter
3 cups sugar
6 eggs
3 cups all-purpose flour
1/4 teaspoon baking soda
pinch of salt
1 cup sour cream

2 teaspoons rum
1 teaspoon orange extract
1/4 teaspoon almond extract
2/3 teaspoon lemon extract
1 teaspoon vanilla extract
1/2 cup peach brandy

Cream butter and gradually add sugar, beating well. Add eggs one at a time, mixing well after each addition. Combine flour, soda and salt; add to creamed mixture alternately with sour cream, beating well after each addition. Stir in remaining ingredients. Pour batter into a well-greased and floured 10-inch Bundt pan or tube pan. Bake at 325 degrees for 1 hour and 20 minutes or until cake tests done.

KATE BUNTING'S SEAFOOD HOUSE
Ocean City

KATE BUNTING'S
SEAFOOD HOUSE

A sign reading "Since 1981" might not suggest a historic restaurant, but turn those numbers around and you'll find that the building at 10 Talbot Street dates back to 1891. At that time, it was a boarding house called the Mount Vernon Inn. In 1981, the yellow Victorian building became Kate Bunting's Seafood House. Mrs. Bunting makes a point of adding "Since 1981" to the restaurant's name because she feels herself a part of the history of downtown Ocean City and wants to help revitalize it.

The "old" Ocean City has a number of small hotels and motels, some of which have been in the same family for years. Kate Bunting's family has a long association with one of them, the Belmont-Hearne. In 1905 Kate's great-grandmother took over the twelve-room Belmont Hotel. Kate's grandmother was married in the lobby (at 6:30 a.m.), and Kate's father was born in the hotel. While Kate was growing up in Pennsylvania, she spent summers at the Belmont. Now her daughter is the manager of the same hotel, just across the way from Kate Bunting's Seafood House.

The restaurant was renovated to look like the original Mt. Vernon Inn depicted on postcards. Those who have remodeled old houses will not be surprised to hear that it took three weeks to redo one stairway alone. The renovation also included extra foundation supports and insulated walls and ceilings. When the house was jacked up, old medicine bottles were found underneath, evidence that a pharmacy occupied the site at one time.

My husband, Gordon, and I drove from Atlantic City to Kate Bunting's on a hot summer day, and our warm reception at the Seafood House included a cool drink. We sat with Kate Bunting on an upstairs porch by branches of a weeping willow and sipped a frozen Melon Colada. If you like Piña Coladas, you'll like this combination of pineapple juice, coconut milk and rum, and the flavor of melon liqueur will make you think you're sipping straight from a honeydew.

As we cooled off on the balcony, we watched groups on the patio below devouring all-you-can-eat steamed crabs.

The hot crabs were served with plenty of beer and lots of paper towels. Crackers and crocks of cheese were on the tables along with melted butter and buckets for shells. Children and their parents went at the crabs with mallets.

The dining room we ate in was decorated with signs and shingles, some with dates, names or addresses, to represent downtown neighbors past and present. There was the Laurel House, Mrs. Bull, Manager, 1890; the Belmont, Circa 1897, Elizabeth H. Hearne, Sole Proprietor; and the U. S. Coast Guard Station, Ocean City, Md., 1878. But Gordon and I were distracted from this historic décor when the chef described his recipe for Stuffed Pork Chops. They tasted as good as they sounded. The chops were filled with seasoned bread stuffing combined with a spicy apple mixture.

The chef also gave us his suggestions for good picnic fare: not fried chicken, but smoked fish and poultry. He insisted that "shark is more like chicken than chicken is."

We liked the sound of Oysters Coleman, named for Kate Bunting's husband, who tired of Oysters Casino. This casserole of oysters with Swiss cheese and bacon is easy to fix when oysters are available. My respects to the chef, but I think I'll choose oysters over shark.

Kate Bunting's Seafood House is located at 10 Talbot Street in Ocean City. Meals are served from 11:00 a.m. until 11:00 p.m., daily. For reservations (accepted) call (301) 289-1441.

KATE BUNTING'S SEAFOOD HOUSE'S
MELON COLADA

crushed ice	**¾ ounce melon liqueur**
½ ounce coconut milk	**¾ ounce rum**
¾ ounce pineapple juice	**stemmed cherry**

Fill a 10-ounce glass with crushed ice. Transfer the ice to blender and add coconut milk, pineapple juice, liqueur and rum. Blend until smooth, pour into glass and top with cherry. Serves 1.

KATE BUNTING'S SEAFOOD HOUSE'S
OYSTERS COLEMAN

1 pint select oysters
1 teaspoon chopped fresh
 garlic

1 tablespoon oil
1/2 pound Swiss cheese
1/2 pound sliced bacon

Lay oysters in a casserole. Combine garlic and oil and pour over oysters. Top with Swiss cheese and quarter-slices of bacon. Bake in a 400-degree oven until bacon is brown. Serves 4.

KATE BUNTING'S SEAFOOD HOUSE'S
STUFFED PORK CHOPS

6 pork chops, at least 1 inch
 thick
salt and pepper
flour for dredging
oil to cover pan
1/2 cup chopped onion
1/2 cup chopped celery

1 1/2 cups seasoned bread
 crumbs
1/2 cup beef and/or chicken
 stock
8 ounces apple pie filling
1/4 teaspoon cinnamon

Cut a slit halfway through the thickness of each pork chop, deep enough to make a pocket. Season chops with salt and pepper. Dredge in flour and brown in hot oil on both sides over medium heat. Remove from pan and set aside. Sauté onion and celery in remaining oil in pan. In a bowl mix onion, celery, bread crumbs and stock. Rinse excess coating from apple pie filling. Sprinkle cinnamon over pie filling and combine with stuffing mixture. Stuff pork chops and bake them in a 325-degree oven for 30 to 45 minutes. Serves 6.

CAPTAIN'S GALLEY
Crisfield

CAPTAIN'S GALLEY

A big red crab painted on the water tower was our advance notice that Crisfield is called the "crab capital of the world." My husband, Gordon, and I drove into town on a Sunday morning to take a ferry to Smith Island. Next to the city dock, I noticed on a sign above a building the words, *The New York Times.* Thinking I might buy a copy of that paper, I walked up to the building. On closer inspection, however, I found that the building was a restaurant called Captain's Galley. *The New York Times* was listed because it had reviewed the restaurant . . . favorably, I might add.

Another sign that hangs over the building reads, "Best Crab Cakes in the World." Since we had time to spare before catching Captain Frank Dize's *Island Belle*, which is also the mail boat, we went into Captain's Galley for a cup of coffee. On the breakfast menu we noticed a "Crabber's Special" of three pancakes, three eggs and a choice of meat. We talked with the owner's son, who said, "Grandmother comes early every morning and makes the Crab Cakes."

We learned that tracks of the Pennsylvania Railroad used to be in the middle of Main Street, built on oyster shells. In the 1930s the restaurant building served as a wholesale fish house, and in the 1940s it was a crab picking plant. Later it became a restaurant.

Since seafood has always provided the main industry in Crisfield, the town would obviously be a good place for someone to relocate if he were retired from his job in Baltimore, had had some experience in the food business, and wanted to live near the water and indulge in his favorite sport of fishing. The person described is Captain James Dodson, who bought the restaurant after reading in a newspaper advertisement that it was for sale. (Encouraged, no doubt, by First Mate Beverly—and their son and daughter, who work at Captain's Galley—and the grandmother who makes the Crab Cakes.) Captain Dodson estimates that he catches (by hook and line, not net) ninety percent of the fish that are served at Captain's Galley.

Gordon and I did ride to Smith Island and back with Captain Dize and enjoyed being on waters charted by Captain John Smith in 1608. We felt that we had been drawn back in time ourselves when we docked at Ewell and walked to another restaurant in a house whose "address" was "the second house beyond the church."

Back in Crisfield, we returned to Captain's Galley for Crabmeat Salad, the good taste of which I remembered for days, and a sampling of the appealing salad bar, made out of an overboard crab float. Large clear bowls were set in ice, with spiced apple rings scattered around them like life preservers. Green and red tomatoes, green and red peppers, green and red beans, radishes that looked like peppermints—these and other salad vegetables and greens were arranged alongside the dressings and loaves of bread.

Before we left Captain's Galley, we read their publicity in the lobby. I agree with what *The New York Times* said: "Anyone who won't eat a crab is one."

Captain's Galley is located at the foot of Main Street in Crisfield. Meals are served from 8:00 a.m. until 10:00 p.m., Sunday through Thursday; from 8:00 a.m. until 11:00 p.m. on Friday and Saturday; and from 7:00 a.m. until 10:00 p.m. on Sunday. For reservations (accepted) call (301) 968-0300 or (301) 968-1636.

CAPTAIN'S GALLEY'S BROILED
BACKFIN CRABMEAT

³/₄ **pound backfin crabmeat**   **3 tablespoons butter**
dash of Old Bay seasoning   **parsley flakes**
¹/₄ **cup sauterne**

Pick out any remaining shells in crabmeat. Place crabmeat in individual casserole dishes. Lightly sprinkle Old Bay seasoning over the crabmeat, and pour 2 tablespoons sauterne over each dish. Dot with butter, sprinkle with parsley flakes, and broil for 10 minutes. Serves 2.

11

CAPTAIN'S GALLEY'S SPICY ONE

3 8- to 10-ounce red snapper
   fillets
1/4 teaspoon salt
1 1/2 teaspoons Old Bay
   seasoning

1 1/2 teaspoons paprika
4 tablespoons lemon juice
1/4 teaspoon parsley flakes
3 tablespoons butter
lemon slices

Place fillets in baking dish, and sprinkle with salt, Old Bay seasoning and paprika. Sprinkle with lemon juice and top with parsley. Dot with butter, and broil for 12 to 15 minutes or until fish flakes easily. Garnish with lemon slices. Serves 3.

CAPTAIN'S GALLEY'S CRABMEAT SALAD

1/2 cup mayonnaise
3/4 teaspoon Old Bay
   seasoning
1/4 teaspoon Worcestershire
   sauce

dash of hot sauce
2 cups backfin crabmeat,
   picked
3/4 cup diced celery

Whisk mayonnaise, Old Bay seasoning, Worcestershire sauce, and hot sauce into a smooth mixture. In a large bowl, gently combine crabmeat and celery. Spoon the mayonnaise mixture over crabmeat, and lightly blend. Serves 4 to 6.

HOTEL INN RESTAURANT AND LOUNGE
THE WASHINGTON HOTEL
Princess Anne

HOTEL INN RESTAURANT

Some people don't believe in coincidence. Was it fate then that brought Gordon and me to meet Mary Murphey, owner of The Washington Hotel, shortly after we had bought an artist's print entitled "Mary Murphy"? Fate seemed compatible with a strong sense of history in the hotel, which has been in continuous operation since 1744.

The lobby has two staircases: one for women in hoopskirts, the other for men. Photographs are segregated, too: U. S. Presidents on one wall, First Ladies on another. We had a room at the top of the stairs where Basil Rathbone spent the night when he appeared in a play at the University of Maryland-Eastern Shore. Some rooms have been modernized, but Mary Murphey says guests prefer old furnishings. She is proud of the family antiques in her living quarters downstairs. From a 1789 ledger she showed us, I learned that two gallons of brandy was considered fair pay for one day's work.

In the Hotel Inn, managed by Mrs. Murphey's son, we were seated in the dining room that honors Judge Samuel Chase, a signer of the Declaration of Independence from the town of Princess Anne. I recognized "a large mahogany sideboard (very valuable)" as being the one listed in a 1900 inventory of furniture, which Mary Murphey had shown us. It was made more valuable for me by holding baskets of Gaillardia daisies flanked by old wine bottles.

A party of sixteen people at one end of the room was offering toasts. I learned that it was a fiftieth wedding anniversary party, a celebration all the more special because the couple had been married at the Washington Hotel.

Our waitress said that the party was being served one of the restaurant's most popular dishes, Seafood Imperial, which was not on the menu that night. We asked if we could have it, too, and were glad we did; it was spicy and full of shrimp.

The Hotel Inn cuisine is local Eastern Shore seafood. Dinners include a salad and two vegetables. We chose four

14

different vegetables and decided that our favorite was the Stewed Tomatoes, with their cinnamon-nutmeg flavor.

As we ate, a young couple was seated near us. He wore a red rose boutonniere and she, an iris corsage. Although I tried not to intrude by staring, I admired their happy good looks and noticed what they ordered: Pecan Pie for him, Blueberry Pie à la Mode for her. Finally I spoke, and my suspicions were confirmed—it was their wedding day. I found it a coincidence that Gordon and I, seated between the newlyweds and the fifty-year celebrants, had been married twenty-five years. To honor that coincidence, we had a dessert with a "wedding" flavor—rice custard.

On Sunday morning, when we were leaving the hotel, I saw on the floor in front of the register a grain of rice, and a flower from the bride's bouquet.

Hotel Inn Restaurant and Lounge is located in the Washington Hotel at 32 Somerset Avenue in Princess Anne. Lunch is served from 11:00 a.m. until 2:00 p.m., Monday through Saturday. Dinner is from 4:30 p.m. until 9:00 p.m., Monday through Saturday. For reservations call (301) 651-2526.

HOTEL INN RESTAURANT AND LOUNGE'S
RICE CUSTARD

4 eggs	¾ cup cooked rice
½ cup sugar	whipped cream
1 quart milk	nutmeg
pinch of salt	cinnamon
1 teaspoon vanilla	

Beat eggs and sugar together. Add milk, salt, vanilla and rice. Bake in a greased 9x13-inch pan for 1 hour at 350 degrees. Serve warm or cold, topped with whipped cream and sprinkled with nutmeg and cinnamon. Serves 10 to 12.

Note: This dish will keep in the refrigerator up to a week.

HOTEL INN RESTAURANT AND LOUNGE'S
STEWED TOMATOES

2 16-ounce cans tomatoes
2 cups sugar
2 teaspoons nutmeg
2 teaspoons cinnamon

3 slices stale bread, cubed
1 tablespoon butter
cornstarch

Mash canned tomatoes in a saucepan. Add sugar, nutmeg, cinnamon, cubed bread and butter. Simmer mixture on top of stove until flavors are well blended. Add cornstarch to thicken as desired. Serves 4 to 6.

HOTEL INN RESTAURANT AND LOUNGE'S
SEAFOOD IMPERIAL

1 egg
1 tablespoon dry mustard
1 tablespoon Old Bay
  seasoning
1 teaspoon Worcestershire
  sauce

3 tablespoons mayonnaise
2 jumbo shrimp (peeled
  and deveined)
1 pound crabmeat

In a bowl, beat the egg and add mustard, Old Bay seasoning, Worcestershire sauce and mayonnaise. Cut shrimp in small pieces and mix into crabmeat. Gently mix crabmeat with egg mixture. Pour into baking dish. Dot with butter and bake in a 350-degree oven for 25 minutes. Serves 4.

THE CHAMBERS
Easton

THE CHAMBERS   "Christmas is coming; the goose is getting fat." I was reminded of the old song my nephew Mark loved to sing when I heard about The Chambers' "Operation Christmas Goose." It has become a tradition for the restaurant to prepare meals of roasted wild geese with stuffing, green beans and sweet potatoes as gifts for the hungry. Local merchants and hunters donate much of the food; The Chambers cooks it; and businessmen help deliver it hot on Christmas Eve.

Easton, called the Colonial Capital of the Eastern Shore, has a heritage of waterfowling and hunting and is home to a famous Waterfowl Festival every fall. Appropriately, the Chambers chose a hunting horn for its logo. Located at Court House Square, the restaurant is in an 1892 building that once housed harness, dry goods and grocery shops.

It was not waterfowl season when I visited The Chambers, so I feasted on seafood. I began with an appetizer of Crab Balls and found the crab crisp and delicious. Then I ordered the chef's specialty, Butterfly Shrimp stuffed with Crab Imperial. The sight of those bubbling, cheesy puffs on an oval platter was unforgettable—and so was the taste.

For cooking waterfowl at home, I took the recipe for Rum Raisin Duck. I like the combination of rum, raisins and honey as a basting sauce to flavor the bird.

The dining rooms at The Chambers are called the Library, the Tavern and the Gallery Room. In the Library, I checked out some of the titles on the nineteenth-century mantelpiece. Some of the books are from the library of one of Talbot County's first magistrates, Judge John C. North. Two I noted were *Maryland Reports* and *Cyclopedia of Law and Procedure.*

In case this kind of reading proves too dry, the Gas Light Bar is in the next room. Dedicated by author James Michener, the bar gets its name from the rare 1885 gas and electric chandelier that is its centerpiece. The gas lanterns are lit on special occasions.

Between the bar and the Library are two front-row seats (7A and 8B) from the Lyric Theater in Baltimore. Under the seats you can see racks made to hold the wide-brimmed hats fashionable in 1898.

It would be fun to dine in various rooms and see all the artifacts, but on my first visit, I chose the Library, where I could imagine *Maryland's Historic Restaurants and Their Recipes* shelved among the venerable old books someday.

The Chambers is located at 22 West Dover Street in Easton. Meals are served from 11:00 a.m. until 9:00 p.m., Monday through Thursday; from 11:00 a.m. until 10:30 p.m., Friday and Saturday; and from 4:00 p.m. until 9:00 p.m. on Sunday. Sandwiches are available until midnight seven days a week. For reservations (accepted) call (301) 822-5521.

THE CHAMBERS' CRAB BALLS

1 egg
4 tablespoons mayonnaise
1½ tablespoons prepared
  yellow mustard
1 pound backfin crabmeat
5 slices white bread

2 tablespoons celery salt
1 tablespoon white pepper
  (or to taste)
2 tablespoons chopped fresh
  parsley
peanut oil

In a bowl, mix egg, mayonnaise and mustard. Add crabmeat, and carefully toss until blended. Whip bread in blender to make crumbs and add to it the celery salt, pepper and parsley. Add bread mixture to crabmeat mixture. Form into small balls, and deep fry in peanut oil heated to 350 degrees until golden brown. Yields 8 appetizer servings.

THE CHAMBERS' RUM RAISIN DUCK

1 Long Island duck,
  approximately 5 pounds
½ cup honey

½ cup rum
⅓ cup raisins

Cut duck in half and put in roasting pan. Combine honey, rum and raisins; heat, but don't boil. Baste duck with sauce while roasting, 15 minutes per pound in a 350-degree oven. Before serving, glaze duck with sauce and drippings from pan. Serves 4 or more.

THE CHAMBERS' BUTTERFLY SHRIMP STUFFED WITH CRAB IMPERIAL

16 large white shrimp
Crab Imperial (recipe below)

topping (recipe below)

Prepare shrimp by removing head, shell and skin (leave tail). With a sharp knife cut underside of shrimp from head to tail. Open each shrimp into a butterfly shape on a baking pan. Top with Crab Imperial and topping, and bake in a 350-degree oven for 12 minutes or until cheese is lightly browned. Serves 4.

Crab Imperial:

1 egg
4 tablespoons mayonnaise
1 teaspoon dry mustard
2 tablespoons Worcestershire sauce

1 tablespoon lemon juice
1 tablespoon Old Bay seasoning
1 pound backfin crabmeat

Mix egg, mayonnaise and mustard. Stir in Worcestershire sauce, lemon juice, and Old Bay seasoning. Add crabmeat, and carefully toss. Place on butterflied shrimp.

Topping:

2 ounces Cheddar cheese
2 ounces Provolone cheese
2/3 cup mayonnaise

1/3 cup egg white
1 tablespoon lemon juice

Shred and blend cheeses, and sprinkle on top of Crab Imperial. Mix mayonnaise, egg white and lemon juice. Pour over cheese and bake as directed above.

ROBERT MORRIS INN
Oxford

ROBERT MORRIS INN

Doesn't everyone look back with regret on some missed opportunity? A friend of mine once had the chance to buy the Robert Morris Inn, but had to pass it up. Things might have been different if he could have borrowed money on his honor, as Robert Morris, Jr., did on his to finance the Continental Army.

The father of that Revolutionary War financier, Robert Morris, Sr., died before the American Revolution, the victim of a freak accident. Wadding from a ship's guns being fired in his honor struck him and proved fatal. The house he lived in is now the Robert Morris Inn. It was built by ships' carpenters before 1710 and bought by an English trading company in 1730 as a residence for Morris, who represented their interests in Oxford.

The Robert Morris Inn is doing well with the motto "Quality is Our Tradition." Innkeepers Wendy and Ken Gibson invite their guests to experience that tradition in a tranquil atmosphere: wonderful food, a reading room, walks by the Tred Avon River or a ride on America's oldest ferry, the Oxford-Bellevue, established in 1683.

Gordon and I ate in the tavern, which has a slate floor, brick booths and the Morris coat of arms over the fireplace. With a glass of good iced tea (never to be taken for granted) in hand, we looked over the menu. Since twenty of twenty-seven entrées were seafood, we ordered a seafood sampler.

The Crab, attractively served on a ruffle of kale, was what we went for first. It was so good that we both saved some for the last bite. We wanted to try Oysters à la Gino, a specialty at the inn, but oysters are not served out of season, and the month of our visit wasn't spelled with an "r." Neither was it the cranberry season when we were there, but the Cranberry Muffins I've since tested are ones I'll bake again.

There is much to admire in the different rooms. Murals in the dining room were made from wallpaper samples used by manufacturers' salesmen one hundred and thirty-five years ago. An enclosed Elizabethan staircase leads to guest rooms, and there are other rooms in Robert Morris Lodge and River

Cottage. The innkeepers say they will decorate every room to their satisfaction—if it takes a lifetime. That's the tradition of quality.

Robert Morris Inn is located on the Tred Avon River at Oxford. Breakfast is served from 8:00 a.m. until 11:00 a.m., daily. Lunch is served from 11:30 a.m. until 4:00 p.m., Monday through Saturday. Dinner is served from 5:00 p.m. until 9:00 p.m., Monday through Saturday. Sunday dinner is served from 1:00 p.m. until 8:00 p.m. Reservations are not accepted, but the telephone number is (301) 226-5111.

ROBERT MORRIS INN'S CRANBERRY MUFFINS

1 cup sifted all-purpose flour	3 ounces orange juice
1/2 cup sugar	1/2 teaspoon grated orange peel
3/4 teaspoon baking powder	1 egg, beaten
1/4 teaspoon baking soda	1/2 cup coarsely chopped fresh cranberries
1/2 teaspoon salt	
2 tablespoons butter	1/4 cup chopped nuts

Preheat oven to 350 degrees. Grease a 12-cup muffin tin. In a large mixing bowl, sift together dry ingredients. Cut in butter. In a separate bowl, combine juice, orange peel and egg. Add to dry ingredients, mixing only enough to moisten. Fold in cranberries and nuts. Fill prepared muffin cups about 2/3 full with batter. Bake for 15 minutes. Cool and wrap overnight. Warm and serve next day. Yields 12 muffins.

ROBERT MORRIS INN'S SCALLOP CASSEROLE

6 tablespoons butter	1/2 teaspoon Old Bay seasoning
1 cup chopped onions	
1 cup chopped celery	1 pound scallops
1 tablespoon basil leaves	1 cup milk
1 teaspoon poultry seasoning	1 tablespoon chopped parsley
1 teaspoon salt	1 1/2 cups bread crumbs
1/2 teaspoon black pepper	

In a heavy skillet, melt 6 tablespoons butter; set aside 2 tablespoons. In remaining butter sauté onions and celery until tender. Add basil, poultry seasoning, salt, pepper and Old Bay seasoning. Add scallops and sauté until tender (approximately 5 minutes) over medium heat, stirring constantly. Add milk and remove from heat. Pour into a medium-sized bowl, sprinkle with parsley, and stir. Add 1 cup of bread crumbs (putting aside remaining ½ cup) and mix well. Put into one 8x8-inch casserole dish or four individual casserole dishes. Mix remaining ½ cup bread crumbs and 2 tablespoons melted butter, stir until moist, and sprinkle on top. Bake in a 350-degree oven for 7 minutes or until golden brown. Serves 4.

ROBERT MORRIS INN'S OYSTERS A LA GINO

2 tablespoons butter
⅓ cup all-purpose flour
1 tablespoon paprika
½ teaspoon monosodium glutamate (optional)
½ teaspoon garlic powder
½ teaspoon Chesapeake Bay-style seafood seasoning
(if not available, add cayenne to other seafood seasoning)

½ teaspoon white pepper
1 cup milk
2 tablespoons Worcestershire sauce
2 tablespoons dry sherry
6 to 8 ounces cooked lump crabmeat (about 1 cup)
24 oysters on the half shell
6 slices bacon, cut into 4 pieces each

Melt butter in a heavy pan over low heat. Mix in flour and dry seasonings. Stir in milk and Worcestershire sauce, and whisk until smooth. Cook until thickened, about 5 minutes, stirring constantly. Remove from heat and add sherry. Cool mixture for 20 minutes. Gently mix in crabmeat. Arrange oysters on a shallow baking pan, and top each with a tablespoon of crab mixture. Place a piece of bacon on top of each. Bake in a 375-degree oven for 10 to 12 minutes or until bacon is crisp. Makes 6 to 8 appetizer servings.

THE PASADENA
Royal Oak

THE PASADENA

Mickey McCrea, The Pasadena's host, met Gordon and me in the entrance hall of the 220-year-old mansion and introduced his mother, his infant daughter, some neighbors and Beauregard, the thirteen-year-old dog who's "been dead twice." We had an instant sense of community, which was made international when we went into the dining room and met two sisters from Germany, one on her first visit to the United States. Their English was better than our German, but Gordon and I do have German surnames to talk about, and there was great gesticulating.

The Pasadena is a conference center owned by Schwaben International, a cultural exchange organization for better world understanding. The historic 135-acre site in Royal Oak provides a place for relaxing and exploring nature, hobbies or customs. The Maryland manager served an apprenticeship in Germany to learn about European-style guest houses.

Even though The Pasadena's building and most of its furnishings are native to Maryland, the rooms have an Old World feeling. Old tools hang on white stucco walls in the parlor, where the floor is covered by a black rug patterned with pink roses and gold leaves. The Lettie Lane family of paper dolls and clothes hang in frames beside a full-length mirror. The dining room has a large, white, built-in cabinet filled with blue and white dishes. Straight-back, spindle chairs with cane seats are pulled around a table for twelve, where meals are served family style.

After a sound sleep in an antique bed, Gordon and I got to the breakfast table too late for company, but not too late for fresh, light Pancakes with bacon and link sausage. There was maple syrup, but I particularly enjoyed the Damson and Fig Preserves, which are served with every meal. At one time forty damson trees grew on Pasadena property. The farm still supplies five acres of fruits and vegetables for the table.

The length of time guests stay at The Pasadena varies from several weeks to just one meal, and menus are planned for particular groups. Bikers on a tour, for instance, might not want red meat and fried foods. Bloomingdale's models have come for years to enjoy water sports and feast on Barbecued Chicken, Spareribs and Fish cooked on a grill.

With no special requests, an average dinner for thirty in the dining room in April would probably include a Fresh Spinach Salad, Crab Imperial (in Lucy's special white sauce) and Sliced Prime Rib or Country Ham, Fig Preserves, Vegetables, and Chocolate Eclairs.

When I left The Pasadena, I took information on Schwaben International flights between New York and Frankfurt. Maybe I could fly to Germany and look up other Scholls and Schencks.

The Pasadena is located on Route 329 in Royal Oak. Meals are served from March through November. Breakfast is served from 8:30 a.m. until 10:00 a.m., and dinner from 6:00 p.m. until 8:00 p.m., Monday through Saturday. Brunch is served from 10:00 a.m. until 1:00 p.m. on Sunday. For reservations (required) call (301) 745-5053.

THE PASADENA'S CRAB IMPERIAL

2 tablespoons butter
2 tablespoons flour
1 cup milk
2 eggs, beaten
2 teaspoons Worcestershire
  sauce

2 teaspoons dry mustard
$1/2$ teaspoon salt
dash of red pepper
1 pound crabmeat
$1/4$ cup bread crumbs
dash of paprika

In a saucepan melt butter and add flour, then milk, stirring to make a smooth white sauce. Add eggs, Worcestershire sauce, mustard, salt and red pepper; pour mixture over crabmeat in a baking dish. Sprinkle bread crumbs and paprika over top, and bake in a 400-degree oven for 30 minutes. Serves 4.

THE PASADENA'S FIG PRESERVES

1 pound ripe figs
1 cup sugar

$1/2$ cup water
$1/2$ lemon, sliced

27

In saucepan bring figs, sugar and water slowly to a boil. Mixture will produce its own syrup. Add lemon slices and simmer for 2 hours. When figs are in a light syrup, remove and seal in scalded jars, or just refrigerate to serve as a complement with meat as well as breads. Keeps well in refrigerator. Yield varies.

THE PASADENA'S DAMSON PRESERVES

1 pound damson plums   1 cup water
1 cup sugar

Boil damsons in sugar and water until fruit splits. Remove seeds, and simmer pulp and juice for 1 to 1½ hours. Scald jars and fill with damsons in a medium syrup; seal. Yield varies.

Note: To increase quantity, use 1 cup sugar per each pound of fruit, with enough water to prevent sticking.

THE PASADENA'S PANCAKES

3 cups all-purpose flour   3 eggs, separated
½ teaspoon salt   2 cups milk
2 teaspoons baking powder   ½ cup butter, melted
½ cup sugar

Sift flour, salt, baking powder, and sugar together into a mixing bowl. In a separate bowl, beat egg yolks and milk, then add to dry ingredients along with the butter. Beat egg whites until stiff and fold into batter. Fry pancakes on hot griddle. Yields 24 4-inch pancakes.

THE INN AT PERRY CABIN
St. Michaels

THE INN AT PERRY CABIN

"**W**e have met the enemy and they are ours," said Commodore Perry after defeating the British in the Battle of Lake Erie. And when the British attacked St. Michaels during the War of 1812, trying to wreck its shipyard, they were outwitted and overshot the town at night because lanterns had been placed in trees.

When Samuel Hambleton built a home in St. Michaels in the early 1800s, he named it Perry Cabin in honor of Commodore Perry, under whom he had served in the U. S. Navy. Although it has a military history, St. Michaels is a peaceful place. It was the home of Amelia Welby, Maryland's Poet Laureate long before Lucille Clifton. James Michener lived there when he wrote *Chesapeake*, and watermen have lived there for centuries. The oyster business that thrived around 1900 is described in *St. Michaels Reminiscences*, written by Edward B. Watkins, whose father "ran an oyster house in the fall and winter, a crab packing plant in the spring, and a tomato cannery in summer."

Today The Inn at Perry Cabin is owned by Harry and Teresa Meyerhoff, who also own prize horses such as Spectacular Bid and Silent King. At one point during its transition from private residence to inn, Perry Cabin was a riding academy. The horse theme is appropriately carried through on the menu, which lists not "Appetizers" and "Desserts," but "Starters" and "Finishers."

Eating in the former carriage house, now called the Spectacular Bid Bar, Gordon and I enjoyed a dinner that would win, place or show. Escargots and Mushroom Caps made a perfect combination to bake in garlic butter. I was grateful to the chef responsible for the spicy goodness of Crab Imperial, and to the watermen responsible for providing the main ingredient. The fishing trade also contributed to the Veal Boloxi, since it was topped with shrimp.

I was able to go only a short distance on Fogg Cove Mile High Pie, but that ice cream creation was a sure winner.

The carriage house looks out on Fogg Cove, and binoculars

30

are furnished for spotting osprey, swans and raccoons. A gazebo at the water's edge lends itself to such celebrations as weddings and Preakness parties.

During the summer, when people vacation on private boats, the inn operates a water taxi, picking up from the harbor or marina customers who call for reservations. Another warm weather benefit is the cruise dinner offered in spring and summer. Guests go aboard a cruise boat to dine and also spend an hour or two seeing estates along the Miles River.

If Pogo could paraphrase Commodore Perry's communiqué, why can't I? We have met The Inn at Perry Cabin, and the recipes are ours.

The Inn at Perry Cabin is located in St. Michaels. Lunch is served from 11:30 a.m. until 4:00 p.m., Monday through Saturday, and from 11:30 a.m. until 3:00 p.m. on Sunday. Dinner is served from 5:30 p.m. until 10:00 p.m., Monday through Thursday; from 5:00 p.m. until 11:00 p.m., Friday and Saturday; and from 3:30 p.m. until 10:00 p.m. on Sunday. For reservations (suggested) call (301) 745-5178.

THE INN AT PERRY CABIN'S CRAB IMPERIAL

1 egg, beaten
1/3 cup mayonnaise
1 teaspoon prepared mustard
1 1/2 teaspoons Worcestershire sauce
1 teaspoon lemon juice
dash of white pepper
1 teaspoon Old Bay seasoning
2 teaspoons diced pimentos
2 teaspoons diced green pepper
3/4 teaspoon sherry
1/2 teaspoon Tabasco sauce
2 teaspoons chopped fresh parsley
1 pound crabmeat
red and green pepper strips for garnish

Thoroughly blend first 12 ingredients. Add crabmeat, gently folding into mixture with spatula. Place mixture in baking shell and criss-cross thin strips of red and green

31

pepper over center for color. Bake in a 350-degree oven until golden brown, approximately 10 minutes. Serves 4.

THE INN AT PERRY CABIN'S VEAL BOLOXI

12 ounces veal cutlet	**2 teaspoons capers**
½ cup clarified butter	**¼ cup white wine**
8 medium-large shrimp,	**½ pound cooked fettuccine**
** peeled and deveined**	**chopped fresh parsley**
4 ounces sliced mushrooms	**lemon wedges**

Pound veal between two pieces of waxed paper until thin. Heat butter in a skillet and add veal. Sauté veal, then add shrimp, mushrooms, capers and wine. Serve over fettuccine, with shrimp arranged on top of veal. Garnish with parsley and lemon wedges. Serves 2.

THE INN AT PERRY CABIN'S ESCARGOTS IN MUSHROOM CAPS

½ pound butter, softened	**½ garlic clove, pressed**
¾ ounce sherry	**24 medium mushrooms**
1½ tablespoons fresh lemon	**24 escargots**
** juice**	
½ tablespoon chopped	
** parsley**	

Blend butter with sherry, lemon juice, parsley and garlic; set aside. Remove stems from mushrooms and place caps upside down on escargot dish. Place one escargot in each mushroom cap and top with a portion of garlic butter to cover. Bake in a 350-degree oven until butter is sizzling, approximately 7 minutes. Yields 24 appetizers.

Note: Do not place mushrooms and escargots together until just before baking or the mushrooms will absorb the flavor of the escargots and the separate flavors will be lost.

HARRISON'S CHESAPEAKE HOUSE
Tilghman Island

HARRISON'S CHESAPEAKE HOUSE

Poet William Stafford says, "The reliable sound of the lawnmower puts a net under the afternoon." I think the hum of ceiling fans on a screened porch provides the same sense of well-being, especially if the listener knows that yeast rolls are rising in the kitchen and fish are being caught nearby for supper.

To enter the screened porch and then the dining room at Harrison's Chesapeake House, guests walk past a sign that asks them to do four things: "Have a good time, remember us pleasantly, speak of us kindly and come back to see us again." The requests are easy to comply with, especially when part of the good time is spent rocking on the porch and talking with Mrs. Harrison—"Miss Alice," whom Senator Barry Goldwater called "the world's greatest hostess."

She talks about the early 1900s (and before) when relatives came to the wharf by steamboat from Baltimore to stay in the family's guest rooms. Summer boarders came by horse and buggy, then by train, and drummers (salesmen) sometimes stayed overnight. Harrison's reputation for old-fashioned, family-style cooking grew until the restaurant was regarded as a prime example of Eastern Shore country cuisine.

The "Buddy Plan" governs sport fishing at Harrison's. It covers, in addition to a night's lodging at the inn (the oldest part built in 1856), a fisherman's breakfast of eggs, bacon and pancakes at 6:00 a.m., a day's fishing (tackle provided) on one of the twelve boats in the Harrison's fleet, and a substantial box lunch of chicken and crab cakes, sandwiches, deviled eggs and cake. If you're lucky, you'll have fish to take home—and Harrison's will clean and pack them.

For dinner, it makes sense to order the Catch of the Day. The day I visited, the catch was Sea Trout, a stronger flavored fish than flounder but milder than bluefish. My serving was thick and white and broiled in lemon butter.

Gordon wanted to taste the Crab Cakes that James Michener praises, and he was pleased to discover that a combination of Fried Chicken and Crab Cakes is the Chesapeake House Specialty. They call it their Eastern Shore Dinner in keeping with a sixty-year-old tradition, and its reputation

34

was upheld that night. We also enjoyed a variety of vegetables, and we learned why diners demand Miss Alice's Yeast Rolls, which she leaves the porch to prepare.

Her son, "Captain Buddy," or Levin Faulkner Harrison III, is the man in charge of the Chesapeake House and the sportfishing charter fleet. He carries on the tradition set by the first Levin Faulkner Harrison's father, who left England to settle on Tilghman Island. Senator Goldwater thought Buddy's father was "the greatest ambassador of humanity I have ever met." The notes I made about Captain Buddy read, "sandy-red hair and moustache, nice accent, likes to make people happy." Like father, like son, like six generations—because there is also a Bud and a little Buddy. No wonder theirs is called the Buddy Plan.

Harrison's Chesapeake House is located at the end of Route 33 on Tilghman Island. Breakfast is served from 6:00 a.m. until 11:00 a.m., daily. Lunch is served from 11:30 a.m. until 4:30 p.m., daily. Dinner is served continuously from noon until 10:00 p.m., daily. Reservations are not necessary, but for information on seasonal closing call (301) 886-2123 or (301) 886-2121.

HARRISON'S CHESAPEAKE HOUSE'S YEAST ROLLS

½ cup milk	1 package yeast
3 tablespoons sugar	¼ cup warm water
3 tablespoons shortening	1 egg, beaten
1 teaspoon salt	3 to 3½ cups all-purpose
½ cup cold water	flour

In a saucepan combine milk, sugar, shortening and salt; heat almost to boiling. Remove from heat, add cold water and set aside.

Dissolve yeast in warm water. Add egg and dissolved yeast to milk mixture. Mix in 3 cups of flour. Add extra flour as needed to make dough workable. Knead well until dough becomes elastic. Put dough in a bowl, cover it with a cloth and set it in a warm place. Let dough rise until it doubles in bulk, about 1½ hours.

35

To form cloverleaf rolls, pinch off small balls of dough; place 3 small balls in each cup of a lightly greased muffin tin, and let rise again. Bake in a 400-degree oven for 15 minutes or until golden brown. Yields 2 dozen rolls.

HARRISON'S CHESAPEAKE HOUSE'S CRAB CAKES

1 tablespoon prepared
  mustard
1 tablespoon mayonnaise
salt and pepper to taste
1 egg, beaten
1 teaspoon chopped fresh
  parsley

¾ teaspoon Old Bay
  seasoning
⅓ cup saltine cracker
  crumbs (or fine bread
  crumbs)
1 pound backfin crabmeat
1 cup shortening

In a large bowl, mix all ingredients except crabmeat and shortening. Add crabmeat, handling carefully so as not to break the lumps. Shape crabmeat mixture into patties and fry in very hot shortening in a heavy skillet. Serves 4.

HARRISON'S CHESAPEAKE HOUSE'S
BROILED SEA TROUT

⅔ cup butter
2 teaspoons lemon juice
salt and pepper to taste
1 medium onion, sliced

2 strips bacon, cut in half
2 sea trout fillets
2 dashes paprika

Melt butter and simmer with lemon juice, salt and pepper. Place 3 slices of onion and 2 half-strips of bacon on each trout. Pour lemon butter over trout, and cook under broiler until lightly browned. Sprinkle with paprika and serve immediately. Serves 2.

KITTY KNIGHT HOUSE
Georgetown

KITTY KNIGHT HOUSE

Does Kitty Knight still keep an eye on her house, built in 1755? Some say she still rocks in a chair there. If so, I'm sure she was delighted with the young women who roomed there during World War II while working in defense plants nearby. They were called "powder monkeys," which seems apropos at spunky Mistress Kitty Knight's place.

According to legend, when the British, led by Sir Admiral George Cockburn, attacked Georgetown in 1813, Kitty Knight was waiting for them with a broom and buckets of scalding water. It's debatable whether she was a heroine or a traitor, since Admiral Cockburn dined at Kitty's that night, but only her house and the one next door were left standing when the British burned Georgetown. An alley that used to separate the two buildings now connects them with a parlor, where the mysterious rocking chair sits. A semi-transparent mirror on the wall shows a faint, painted image of Kitty's face.

Reportedly, the house next door to Kitty's served as an Underground Railroad station. Now it is the Admiral Cockburn Tavern, presided over by Bucky, who, like the bartenders of legend, dispenses tidbits of information as he deftly mixes drinks. A disc jockey plays the latest tunes in the Tavern on weekends. At other times the juke box and the cash register make the only music.

There are a dozen rooms for lodging. I slept in a light blue room facing the river. My bed was iron, but some are brass. Other beds are actually converted horse-drawn sleighs.

In the fall and winter, the owner of Kitty Knight House becomes a guide for hunting parties. The busiest months, though, are July and August, when people vacation, often arriving by boat on the Sassafras River.

The restaurant serves Chesapeake seafood in an early American atmosphere. In the main dining room, which overlooks the water, a good salad bar sits inside a skiff. On each table is a wicker basket filled with six rows of breads: Fruit, Apple Butter, Garlic, Sticky Buns, White and Whole Wheat Rolls. The Fruit Bread offered varies from Orange to

Cranberry to Lemon. I enjoyed my Orange Bread because I am partial to the texture and the taste of citrus rind, whether it comes as candied peel at Christmas time or as a bonus in the bread basket.

Kitty Knight House French-fries vegetables that I haven't seen French-fried before—carrots, asparagus and green pepper strips as well as onions and tomatoes. It's fun to see bright green and orange when you bite into the crispy batter. Other vegetables on the menu are Murphy Potato Skins, Sweet Potatoes, Zucchini, and my favorite, Creamed Turnips. (I agree with James J. Kilpatrick that the turnip would be a good national food.)

Paul Masson wine is served by the glass, liter or half-liter. But most folks finish with a slice of fresh-baked pie, then head for the Tavern's music and the shingle that says, "Drinks by Appt. Only."

With no British in sight, I left the Kitty Knight House, but not before I rocked for a minute in that chair.

Kitty Knight House is located on Route 213 in Georgetown. Dinner is served from 5:00 p.m. until 9:00 p.m., Monday through Thursday; from 5:00 p.m. until 10:00 p.m., Friday and Saturday; and from 2:00 p.m. until 9:00 p.m. on Sunday. For reservations (required for large parties) call (301) 648-5305.

KITTY KNIGHT HOUSE'S CRAB BISQUE

1 10-ounce can split pea soup

1 10-ounce can cream of tomato soup

1 cup milk

1/4 cup sherry

1 teaspoon Worcestershire sauce

1/4 teaspoon Old Bay seasoning

4 ounces crabmeat

Combine soups with other liquids and spices in saucepan, stirring over heat until mixture is smooth. Add crabmeat and heat thoroughly. (Water may be added if thinner consistency is desired.) Serves 4.

KITTY KNIGHT HOUSE'S FRENCH-FRIED VEGETABLES

1 egg
1 cup milk
1 cup flour
1/2 6-ounce box seasoned
  croutons
1 green pepper

2 carrots
1 tomato
1 onion
vegetable oil for deep
  frying

Make an assembly line of three bowls followed by a deep fat fryer. Beat egg and milk together in first bowl, and place flour in second bowl. With a rolling pin, mash croutons into crumbs and place in third bowl. Cut vegetables in a variety of sizes and shapes: pepper in strips, carrots crosswise, etc. Dip each piece of vegetable into bowls in the following order: egg wash, flour, egg wash again, and croutons. Then deep fry in oil until coating is evenly browned. Serves 2 or more.

KITTY KNIGHT HOUSE'S ORANGE BREAD

2 medium oranges (seedless
  or with seeds removed)
2 eggs
1/2 cup oil
1/2 cup water

2 cups all-purpose flour
1 1/2 cups sugar
3/4 teaspoon baking powder
3/4 teaspoon baking soda
1/4 teaspoon salt

Grind two oranges and set aside (rind, pulp and juice should weigh 3/4 pound). Mix eggs, oil and water; then add the dry ingredients. Add the ground oranges, stirring batter until well mixed. Pour into a greased and floured 9x13-inch pan, and bake at 350 degrees for 30 minutes or until tester comes out clean. Yields approximately 24 2-inch squares.

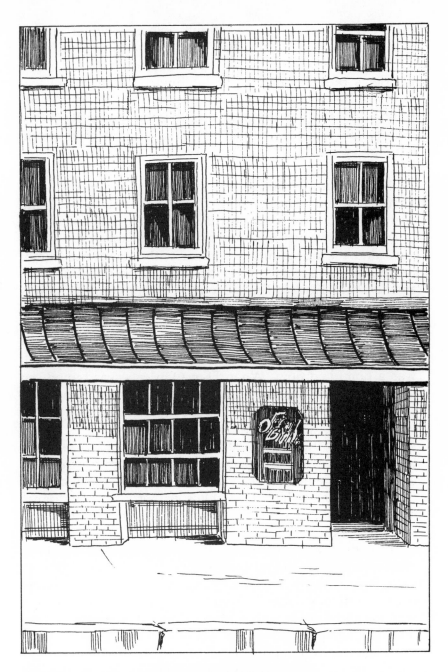

FRAN O'BRIEN'S
Annapolis

FRAN O'BRIEN'S   You'd expect a lot of "firsts" from one of the oldest buildings in Annapolis, and Fran O'Brien's provides them. The building on Main Street was built in 1774. When it was Sam's Cafe in 1936, it was the only dining-and-dancing establishment in town. As La Rosa Restaurant and Lounge in 1948, it made the first pizza pie in Annapolis; and in 1964 it became an inn that featured the first cabaret theatre.

Now, as Fran O'Brien's, it's a dining and dancing establishment again. The restaurant offers American beef and seafood, and a live band provides music for dancing.

The music brings in young people from the Naval Academy, and the restaurant is popular with legislators. Rumor has it that more legislation is enacted at Fran O'Brien's than at the State House. Sure enough, several representatives were there when Gordon and I dined at the restaurant.

In recent years the building was extensively damaged by a fire that started mysteriously in a second floor office, the same location where another fire started years ago when it was a hotel bedroom. When Fran O'Brien's was remodeled after the second fire, the building regained some of the early architectural features that had been altered through the years, such as dormer windows and a tin roof.

I admired the newly redecorated interior. Wood and leaded glass partitions separated the front room bar from the dining room, where tables were covered with peach-colored cloths, and chairs had dark green leather seats. The dance floor was between a salad bar at the end of the dining room and the booth where Gordon and I sat.

Our wine, a Johannisberg Riesling, Ste. Michelle from Washington state, might have inspired us to dance, but we were busy with the Fisherman's Catch of the Day—Grouper baked with a wonderful Seafood Stuffing of shrimp and scallops and topped with a Mustard Sauce. With it came big Stuffed Baked Potatoes, cut across the top, emptied, and filled again with potato, cheese, chives and bacon.

I hesitate to say what dessert we ordered, but its name is

self-explanatory: Coconut Lust. A walnut crust supported creamy, cool layers of yellow and white. On the strength (or weakness) of such a pudding, we waltzed out to Main Street.

Fran O'Brien's is located at 113 Main Street in Annapolis. Lunch is served from 11:30 a.m. until 3:30 p.m., and dinner is from 5:00 p.m. until 10:30 p.m., daily. The band plays from 9:00 p.m. until 1:30 a.m., seven nights a week. For reservations (recommended) call (301) 268-6288.

FRAN O'BRIEN'S COCONUT LUST

Crust:

1 cup all-purpose flour	**1 tablespoon sugar**
1/4 pound (1 stick) margarine	**1 cup chopped walnuts**

Combine above ingredients and press mixture into bottom of baking dish (approximately 9x11 inches). Bake in a 350-degree oven for 30 minutes or until golden brown. Cool before filling.

Cream Cheese Filling:

8 ounces cream cheese	**1 cup non-dairy whipped**
1 cup powdered sugar	**topping**

Blend cream cheese and powdered sugar, and fold in whipped topping. Spread mixture on cooled crust.

Pudding Filling:

1 package instant vanilla pudding	**2 1/2 cups non-dairy whipped topping**
1 cup coconut	**1/3 cup coconut, toasted**

Prepare pudding according to package directions, and add coconut (untoasted). Spread on top of cream cheese mixture. Spread whipped topping on pudding, and sprinkle with toasted coconut. Refrigerate until ready to serve. Serves 8.

43

FRAN O'BRIEN'S SEAFOOD STUFFING

1 pound fresh shrimp,
  chopped
1 pound fresh bay scallops
4 tablespoons butter
¼ cup chopped onion
½ bunch fresh parsley,
  chopped

1 teaspoon Old Bay
  seasoning
4 fish fillets (grouper,
  snapper or flounder)
Mustard Sauce (recipe
  below)

Sauté shrimp and scallops in butter with onion, parsley and Old Bay seasoning. When completely cooked, drain. Stuff into fish or put on top, and top with Mustard Sauce.

Mustard Sauce:
1 egg
1 cup mayonnaise
2 tablespoons prepared
  yellow mustard

½ teaspoon lemon pepper
¼ teaspoon Old Bay
  seasoning
1½ teaspoons sherry

Beat egg and use only half of it for this amount of sauce. Blend all ingredients with a whisk. Spread enough Mustard Sauce on top of Seafood Stuffing to cover fish. Bake in a 400-degree oven for 25 minutes or until fish is done and topping is lightly browned. Serves 4.

FRAN O'BRIEN'S STUFFED BAKED POTATOES

6 large potatoes
¼ pound (1 stick) butter
1 cup milk
3 strips bacon, fried and
  crumbled
1 tablespoon chives

4 tablespoons Cheddar
  cheese soup or sauce
dash of white pepper
salt to taste
dash of mace
paprika

Bake potatoes until done. Cut each one across the very top and scoop out potato pulp. Heat butter with milk, and blend into hot potato pulp. Add remaining ingredients except paprika and beat until smooth. Stuff mixture back into potato skins, sprinkle with paprika and bake in a 375-degree oven for 20 minutes or until golden brown. Serves 6.

HARRY BROWNE'S
Annapolis

HARRY BROWNE'S

A red rose tied with an ominous black ribbon was delivered to Baltimore lawyer Jay Schwartz one day when he was eating lunch at Harry Browne's. At that time, Schwartz was lobbying in the Maryland General Assembly for a controversial bill. The "gift" of the rose upset him, since it was a *Godfather* symbol of death. Excitement spread to the newspapers, and Harry Browne's made headlines. Then it was discovered that several members of the Assembly were just playing a joke on a friend.

Maryland legislators meet now in the State House on the same hallowed ground where George Washington resigned his commission as Commander-in-Chief of the Continental Army in 1783. Annapolis is a model of town planning, and streets radiate from circles named Church and State. The State House, of course, is on State Circle.

It sits on a hill across from Harry Browne's, so the restaurant is a convenient place for legislators to eat; and the Jay Schwartz is a popular sandwich. I ate one the day Gordon and I stopped in for lunch. The warm croissant filled with rare roast beef, almonds and cheese gets my vote.

We didn't receive any red roses, but we did order a good red wine, Marquisat Beaujolais. With it, Gordon enjoyed Harry Browne's Welsh Rarebit, a spicy cheese sauce cooked with beer and served over bacon on toast. We were told that dinner menu favorites include Duck à l'Orange and Sautéed Chicken with fresh vegetables.

We sat at the bar, embellished by an antique breakfront, and sampled Oysters Browne—oysters on the half shell topped with strips of ham and cheese and baked with just a dash of paprika. Owner Rusty Romo showed us a recipe used at the Naval Academy, which calls for three pounds of paprika in Crab Imperial for Four Thousand (hungry midshipmen).

Why would a man named Rusty Romo call a restaurant Harry Browne's? He named it for a favorite uncle. "Everybody has one . . . who always has a couple bucks to give you. You had one," Rusty said. (Yes, I had one; my Uncle

Clyde always wanted to be sure we had a nickel for a Coke.) Rusty's uncle was a builder whose passion was gourmet cooking. Uncle Harry would surely be pleased with both the construction and the continental (American and French) menu of Harry Browne's.

The building has also served as a tannery, an inn, a bank and a tailor's shop. Now it is a restaurant with the air of a neighborhood bar, a 1920s speakeasy lounge with a silhouetted *Great Gatsby*-era couple as its logo. One wall is lined with old photographs, and down the center of the room hang interesting light fixtures salvaged from the *Normandie*, which sank in 1944 and stayed underwater a year and a half in New York Harbor. The chandelier was in the ship's ballroom foyer, and the Zodiac lights hung in the first class dining salon.

Rusty Romo says his uncle used to enter restaurants through the back door because the food, the chef and the kitchen were what interested him the most. If he could visit Harry Browne's today, he'd find plenty to interest him in his nephew's restaurant.

Harry Browne's is located at 66 State Circle in Annapolis. Lunch is served from 11:00 a.m. until 3:30 p.m., Monday through Saturday. Brunch is served from 10:00 a.m. until 3:00 p.m. on Sunday. Dinner is served from 5:00 p.m. until 11:00 p.m., Sunday through Thursday, and from 5:00 p.m. until midnight, Friday and Saturday. For reservations (accepted) call (301) 263-4332.

HARRY BROWNE'S JAY SCHWARTZ

2 croissants
8 to 10 ounces top round roast beef, rare to medium rare, thinly sliced

½ cup sliced almonds
¼ cup Parmesan cheese

Split croissants almost in half, and fill each with 4 to 5 ounces of roast beef, half of the almonds and half of the Parmesan cheese. Warm croissants and serve. Serves 2.

47

HARRY BROWNE'S OYSTERS BROWNE

**1 dozen shucked fresh
oysters, on half shells
2 slices baked ham**

**6 ounces Provolone cheese
dash of paprika
lemon wedges**

Lay oysters on half shells in baking dish. Cut ham in pieces of a size to fit over oysters, and place a piece on each oyster. Divide the cheese into equal portions, and top each ham piece with a half-moon slice of cheese. Sprinkle with paprika. Bake in a 350- to 375-degree oven for 4 to 5 minutes or until cheese browns. Serve 6 oysters on each plate, with lemon wedges. Serves 2 as an appetizer.

HARRY BROWNE'S WELSH RAREBIT

**12 half-strips bacon
4 cups grated Cheddar
cheese
2 cups grated American
cheese
1/4 cup Grey Poupon
mustard
1 1/2 tablespoons
Worcestershire sauce**

**1/8 teaspoon Louisiana hot
sauce
2 eggs, beaten
1/4 cup flour
2/3 cup beer
1/3 cup half and half
12 slices bread**

Fry bacon until crisp. Drain and set aside. In the top of a double boiler combine cheeses with mustard, sauces, eggs and flour, stirring constantly. Add beer and half and half. Stir until thoroughly heated and blended.

Toast 6 slices of bread and lay them in bottom of 6 individual casserole dishes. Top each slice with 2 half-strips of cooked bacon. Cover with sauce, and bake in a 375-degree oven for about 5 minutes. Cut remaining 6 slices of bread in half diagonally, toast them, and serve as toast points, one on each side of each casserole dish. Serves 6.

McGARVEY'S SALOON & OYSTER BAR
Annapolis

McGARVEY'S

I would be drawn to McGarvey's Saloon by its looks alone. The narrow brick building has a symmetrical storefront that shows green café curtains hanging from brass railings. A figure 8 (its street address) is stationed over the front door, and a green "McGarvey's" sign is mounted over that, centering neat architectural brackets. That's the way a saloon should look.

The building has functioned as a saloon since 1871 except during Prohibition, whereas the adjacent wooden building had never been an oyster bar until it became an addition to McGarvey's Saloon. As I stood on the sidewalk and talked to the owner and the chef, a neighboring restaurateur passed us and jokingly warned, "She pulled this on us yesterday!"

Hanging beside the bar is a plaque from members of "The Annapolis Marching, Chowder and Drinking Society," expressing their sober appreciation to owner Mike Ashford for establishing McGarvey's Saloon and wishing him good luck. I was there on the ninth anniversary of that venture, and obviously the owner had been lucky. He attributes that luck to an important location on the city dock, the "really good people" who work for him, a loyal local clientele, and traffic from the Intracoastal Waterway.

Mike Ashford welcomes Waterway travelers. He himself traveled for twenty years as an airline pilot. He took mental pictures of things he liked and noted the places that stood the test of time, such as Third Avenue bars in New York. He admired the Oyster Bar at Grand Central Station, with its individual steam heating pots. They influenced him when he turned an 1812 tobacco warehouse into McGarvey's Oyster Bar.

Lunching in the Oyster Bar, I found the interior bright and contemporary, with skylights, trees growing through grates in white tile squares, and sun patterns on wood. Mike Ashford ordered Baby Beef Liver and Onions, the chef's special for the day. I enjoyed Shrimp James, an unexpected combination of shrimp and spaghetti sauce. That dish has sentimental value, because it was named for a manager's two-year-old son.

50

The chef is a peruser of books, going to the library for new ideas just as he goes to the market for fresh produce each morning before deciding on specials for lunch and dinner. On a hot day he might serve Cold Zucchini Soup or Split Pea with Mint. I was fortunate to get the recipe that had just won first place in the Annapolis Original Crab Soup Contest: Crab, Asparagus and Cheddar Cheese Soup.

McGarvey's honors its good friend Walter Cronkite by naming an eight-ounce sirloin "Captain Cronkite's Steak." It is served with chili and chopped onions on the side. Mike Ashford, a sailor also, says a sailors' rendezvous calls for ice cold beer and a bowl of chili. After being denied such food in travel, he wants to get back to basics: a good cheeseburger, a grilled peanut butter and jelly.

McGarvey's Saloon & Oyster Bar is located at 8 Market Space in Annapolis. McGarvey's serves the full menu from 11:00 a.m. until 1:00 a.m., daily, and the bar is open until 2:00 a.m., daily. Brunch is served from 10:00 a.m. until 2:00 p.m., Saturday and Sunday. Reservations are not accepted, but the phone number is (301) 263-5700.

McGARVEY'S SALOON & OYSTER BAR'S CRAB, ASPARAGUS, AND CHEDDAR CHEESE SOUP

³/₄ cup butter	1 rib celery, chopped fine
³/₄ cup flour	¹/₄ cup onion, chopped fine
1 quart chicken stock	1 pound Cheddar cheese,
¹/₂ pound bacon, cooked	shredded
crisp and crumbled	1 quart half and half
2 pounds asparagus,	1 pound backfin crabmeat
steamed, chopped fine	

In a heavy skillet melt butter, add flour and stir over moderate heat to make a golden roux. Set aside. Combine chicken stock with bacon, asparagus, celery and onion. Bring to a boil. Add cheese, and thicken with roux. Cool, then add half and half. Add crabmeat last. Rest at least six hours, preferably overnight. Reheat before serving. Serves 6 to 8.

51

McGARVEY'S SALOON & OYSTER BAR'S
SHRIMP JAMES

1/4 cup oil
1 1/2 pounds shrimp, peeled
4 cups spaghetti sauce
   (commercial or
   homemade)

3/4 pound Feta cheese
French bread

Heat oil. Add shrimp and heat through. Add spaghetti sauce, and cook shrimp in sauce for 5 to 8 minutes. Add half the Feta cheese, crumbled. When cheese is melted, pour mixture in boats or plates, crumbling the remaining cheese on top. Serve with French bread for dipping. Serves 4.

McGARVEY'S SALOON & OYSTER BAR'S
OYSTER CORN CHOWDER

1 medium onion, chopped
1 16-ounce can cream-style
   corn
1 pint milk

2 ounces ham, chopped fine
1 pint oysters, with liquor

In a soup pot, combine first four ingredients and heat thoroughly. Add oysters and simmer for 5 minutes. Yields 6 cups.

McGARVEY'S SALOON & OYSTER BAR'S
ANNAPOLITAN SANDWICH

2 tablespoons butter
2 green peppers, sliced
1/2 medium onion, sliced
1 loaf French bread,
   quartered

1 pound corned beef, sliced
8 slices tomato
8 slices Swiss cheese

Melt butter and sauté peppers and onion until just tender. Cut bread in half lengthwise. On bottom half of bread, layer corned beef, peppers and onions, and slices of tomato. Top with cheese, cover with top half of bread, and wrap in foil. Heat in oven until cheese is melted. Serves 4.

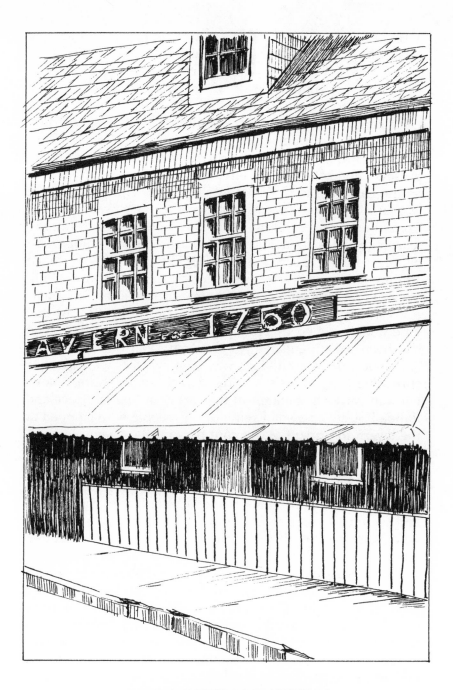

MIDDLETON TAVERN
Annapolis

MIDDLETON TAVERN

I t's fun sometimes to sit in a very old building and think about the famous people from history who have sat right where you are. Middleton Tavern is a good place for such thoughts.

If history recorded *you* as a famous person, what account would it give of your comings and goings? Thomas Jefferson's records note that in 1783 he gave Samuel Middleton passage money to ride the ferry from Annapolis to Rock Hall on the Eastern Shore. We know, then, that Thomas Jefferson was at Middleton Tavern, because the ferry was operated from the tavern building. That ferry offered all the more reason (besides food and lodging) for history's important people to have been guests at Middleton Tavern. Tench Tilghman, for instance, used the ferry in carrying to Philadelphia the message of Cornwallis' surrender at Yorktown.

President James Monroe visited the tavern in 1818. At that time it was owned by Annapolis Mayor John Randall, who had been a distinguished Revolutionary War officer.

At one time the building was a showplace, with gardens spreading from Prince George Street to the water. Now, without gardens, it stands at the corner of Market Space and Randall Street as a solid reminder of people who stopped at the tavern in pursuit of our country's business and pleasure.

When Horatio Middleton acquired the tavern in 1750, he operated it as an Inn for Sea Faring Men. I thought of that as I ate a Middleton Tavern meal symbolic of traveling the high seas: Cuban Black Bean Soup and Lobster Luicci, Irish Coffee and Grand Marnier. It was beautifully served by a manager who said he loved the "extra" touches—melted butter, orange slices and parsley.

He expertly divided dishes for Gordon and me tableside so that we could sample Crab Middleton and Lobster Luicci, both served with toast points. The crab was a sensory delight—I could *see* the pimento and *taste* the lemon. I thought the Lobster Luicci was the best lobster I've ever tasted—thanks, I think, to the tarragon butter baked on the lobster's breading.

Cuban Black Bean Soup I've had before, and I love the combination of rice underneath it, chopped onions on top. Middleton Tavern serves cups of rice and onion on a plate to the side of the soup, so a diner may add as much as he wishes. This soup is not puréed; it's thick with whole black (or turtle) beans, and simmered a long time with seasonings and green peppers, onions and celery.

Who can resist vanilla ice cream when it comes in a square chocolate cup filled also with wonderful strawberries, whipped cream and slivered almonds? But we considered our real dessert to be the Irish Coffee. It must have tasted more authentic because the present owner of Middleton Tavern got the recipe in Ireland, from the Irish Ambassador.

The crowning touch of the manager's "extras" was a sip of Grand Marnier that was 150 years old. That made *me* feel like a famous person.

Middleton Tavern is located at 2 Market Space in Annapolis. Meals are served from 11:30 a.m. until 10:00 p.m., Monday through Friday, and from 11:00 a.m. until midnight on Saturday and Sunday. For reservations (accepted for priority seating) call (301) 263-3323.

MIDDLETON TAVERN'S
CUBAN BLACK BEAN SOUP

1 pound black (turtle) beans	½ teaspoon black pepper
¼ cup bacon grease	1½ teaspoons salt
½ cup chopped celery	1 teaspoon cumin
½ cup chopped onions	1 teaspoon oregano leaves
½ cup chopped green peppers	1 cup rice
	1 large onion, chopped

Place beans in hot water to cover and soak for 2 hours, then parboil in the same water for 15 minutes. Pour off that water to remove acid. Rinse and cover beans with 2 quarts cold water. In a separate pan, heat bacon grease and sauté celery, onions and peppers. Add sautéed vegetables to beans. Add

55

pepper, salt, cumin and oregano. Simmer, stirring occasionally, for 4 hours or until beans are tender. Serve cooked rice and chopped onion as accompaniments. Serves 8.

MIDDLETON TAVERN'S IRISH COFFEE

1 ounce Irish whiskey
1 ounce coffee liqueur
4 ounces coffee

1 ounce whipped cream
cinnamon sprinkles

Combine whiskey and liqueur with coffee in glass. Place whipped cream on top, and decorate with cinnamon sprinkles. Serves 1.

MIDDLETON TAVERN'S LOBSTER LUICCI

1 lobster tail
1 tablespoon oil
1 garlic clove, chopped
¼ cup Burgundy

1½ teaspoons dried tarragon
¼ cup butter
1 egg, beaten
½ cup bread crumbs

Cut lobster tail out of shell. Cross-cut tissues so it does not curl. In a skillet, heat oil and sauté garlic until opaque. Add Burgundy and tarragon, and cook until Burgundy disappears. Add butter, stirring until it is melted and all flavors are incorporated. Dip lobster in egg and coat with bread crumbs. Place in a baking dish and pour tarragon butter over lobster. Bake in a 375-degree oven for 6 to 8 minutes. Serves 1.

RIORDAN'S SALOON
Annapolis

RIORDAN'S SALOON **I**t was so crowded in Riordan's Saloon on one recent St. Patrick's Day that it took a while to notice the Clydesdale horse (visiting Annapolis for the Spring Festival). It came in the back door and stood—head over the rail, other end out the door—drinking a bucket of green beer.

In the 1890s, when horses were a more common sight on the streets, Riordan's was a residence. Later, officers from visiting ships and the U. S. Naval Academy rented rooms on the second and third floors. The first floor is remembered as a produce market that supplied ships in Severn-Annapolis Harbor. The store expanded to include drugstore items and then hardware before it became a clothing store.

Today, antique signs for cigars and whiskey are part of Riordan's décor, purchased by someone on the staff with an eye for auctions. Also on the wall is a caricature of Mike Riordan, dressed to play ball for the Washington Bullets, before he traded that profession for the restaurant business.

Riordan's food is American, with an accent on sauces for seafood. One of the favorite Sunday brunch dishes is Seafood Mornay Randell, named for a chef. With two good cheeses, scallops, crabmeat and shrimp, it's easy to see why the dish is popular. The barbecue sauce on Maryland Bar-B-Que Shrimp is also used on Swordfish and Pineapple Kabobs.

I asked for the recipe for the veggie entrée that I enjoyed: a zucchini casserole, colorful with Eastern Shore cherry tomatoes and spicy with dill weed. It's called Brad's Choice, and I would choose it again, too.

Although seamen no longer live on the second floor of Riordan's, they can eat Maryland Lady Crab Cakes there by candlelight on Friday and Saturday nights. The first floor doesn't sell or dry clean clothes, as it once did, but you can get a Maryland Lady Crab Cake Sandwich or other quick meals downstairs.

If I were at Riordan's on St. Patrick's Day, I'd order Lamb Stew with Soda Bread, and of course, Corned Beef and

Cabbage. I'd hate to overlook an Irish Hero, and I'd try the beer if it were the right shade of green. With enough of that, maybe I would see a Clydesdale horse.

Riordan's is located at 26 Market Space in Annapolis. Meals are served from 11:00 a.m. until 1:00 a.m., Monday through Saturday, and from 10:00 a.m. until 1:00 a.m. on Sunday. Reservations are not accepted for downstairs dining. Dinner is served on Riordan's Second Floor from 6:00 p.m. until midnight, Friday and Saturday. For reservations (strongly recommended) call (301) 263-5449.

RIORDAN'S SALOON'S BRAD'S CHOICE ZUCCHINI CASSEROLE

¼ pound (1 stick) butter
½ cup chopped onions
2 fresh garlic cloves, crushed
3 to 4 medium zucchini, sliced
salt and pepper to taste
1 teaspoon dill weed
1 pint cherry tomatoes
8 ounces Cheddar cheese, cubed
1 cup Italian-seasoned bread crumbs

Heat butter in a skillet and sauté onions and garlic. Add zucchini, salt, pepper and dill weed. Sauté for 5 minutes and reserve the liquid. Layer zucchini with tomatoes and cheese in a 3-quart buttered dish. Combine bread crumbs with half the reserved liquid. Sprinkle over the casserole. Bake uncovered in a 350-degree oven for 25 minutes. Serves 8.

RIORDAN'S SALOON'S SEAFOOD MORNAY RANDELL

2 tablespoons butter
¼ cup flour
2 cups milk
2 tablespoons fresh Romano cheese, grated
4 ounces Gruyère cheese, grated
1 pound bay scallops
16 to 20 medium shrimp, peeled and deveined
1 cup white wine
½ pound lump crabmeat

Melt butter in a saucepan, and add flour to make a roux. Add milk, stirring constantly. Just before mixture reaches boiling point, reduce heat to medium. Add Romano cheese, stirring constantly. When Romano is dissolved, add Gruyère, stirring constantly. Let simmer 5 to 10 minutes, stirring until thickened. While Mornay Sauce simmers, poach scallops and shrimp in wine for 5 to 7 minutes. Drain wine and add sauce and crabmeat. Simmer for 2 to 4 minutes. Serves 4.

RIORDAN'S SALOON'S MARYLAND BAR-B-QUE SHRIMP

Sauce:

1 medium onion, finely chopped	**4 tablespoons brown sauce, commercial or homemade**
2 teaspoons butter	**1½ tablespoons vinegar**
1½ cups catsup	**¾ teaspoon dry mustard**
⅓ cup water	**6 dashes Tabasco sauce**
4 tablespoons Worcestershire sauce	**2 teaspoons tomato paste**

In a large skillet, sauté onions in butter. Add remaining ingredients and simmer, covered, for 20 minutes.

36 large shrimp   **18 strips bacon**

Peel shrimp, leaving tail if desired. Wrap each shrimp in ½ strip of bacon. Place shrimp in baking pan, and bake in a 450-degree oven for 20 to 25 minutes or until bacon is brown. Drain off most of the bacon drippings, and cover shrimp with sauce. Return pan to oven to allow sauce to heat (3 to 5 minutes). Serves 6.

THE TREATY OF PARIS RESTAURANT
MARYLAND INN
Annapolis

THE TREATY OF PARIS RESTAURANT

An amusing thing happened when Bob Denver, of "Gilligan's Island" fame, stayed at Maryland Inn. It took five people to deliver a club sandwich to his room. They marched from the elevator with trays held high, one with a glass of water, another a napkin, then silverware, potato chips and finally the sandwich he'd ordered from room service. These five were the day crew from The Treaty of Paris Restaurant. Frustrated because Denver dined downstairs only in the evening when they couldn't meet him, they saw their chance and took it. And they got autographed pictures for their ingenuity.

Maryland Inn stands on the choice, wedge-shaped lot on Church Circle that was laid out for the use of the town drummer (town crier) in 1694, when the capital moved to Annapolis from Saint Mary's City. An earlier inn on that corner was advertised in a *Maryland Gazette* of the 1780s as "an elegant brick house in a dry and healthy part of the city."

Gordon and I spent a night on Maryland Inn's third floor. There we experienced some of the luxury of the past—spacious quarters, fine antique furniture, and beautiful walnut banisters and other original woodwork.

There is a feeling of history in The Treaty of Paris (named after the document that marked the ending of the Revolutionary War). I sat by a deep-set window, partially below street level, and looked around the room at brick walls decorated with hunting scenes and lanterns. The low-ceilinged room is cozy, with a fireplace at one end. I could imagine a day when early American favorites like Corn Sticks and Popovers—now also favorites at The Treaty of Paris—would have been cooked in that fireplace.

I soon got caught up in reading the wine list—interesting reading, when there are descriptions like "a white wine made from red grapes with a unique copper cast the same shade as the eyes of a black swan. . . ." We settled on a Byrd Gewurztraminer from Maryland and ordered Empanadas for an appetizer. The Spanish "little hats" are puff pastry filled with diced tenderloin of beef, spices and the surprise of brandied raisins.

The Annapolitan Salad—artichoke hearts and shrimp on a bed of Romaine and red leaf lettuce, covered with Green Goddess Dressing—was a treat to watch being prepared tableside. It proved to be even more of a treat to taste.

Eager to try the restaurant's number one entrée, I ordered the Veal Oskar. This classic veal with crabmeat, white asparagus and Béarnaise sauce deserves every bit of its fine reputation. Gordon tried the Treaty of Paris entrée—scallops, shrimp, lobster, oysters and clams in wine, herbs and cream.

After dividing a slice of Grand Marnier Cake, we made a pact to return to The Treaty of Paris.

The Treaty of Paris Restaurant is located in Maryland Inn on Church Circle in Annapolis. Breakfast is served from 7:00 a.m. until 10:45 a.m., daily. Lunch is served from 11:30 a.m. until 3:00 p.m., daily. Dinner is served from 6:00 p.m. until 10:00 p.m., Sunday through Thursday, and from 6:00 p.m. until 11:00 p.m. on Friday and Saturday. For reservations (requested) call (301) 263-2641.

THE TREATY OF PARIS RESTAURANT'S
ANNAPOLITAN SALAD

1 bunch Romaine lettuce
1 head red leaf lettuce
4 artichoke hearts
**24 small to medium shrimp,
  cooked**

**Green Goddess Dressing
(recipe below)**

Arrange lettuces on salad plates. Quarter artichoke hearts and place 4 quarters on each plate with 6 shrimp. Cover with dollops of dressing. Serves 4.

Green Goddess Dressing:
2 cups mayonnaise
½ bunch scallions, diced
1 tablespoon chives
**1 tablespoon chopped
  parsley**

1 tablespoon tarragon leaves
3 anchovies, mashed

Combine ingredients thoroughly, mixing with a whisk. Yields 1 pint.

Note: This dressing keeps well in refrigerator.

THE TREATY OF PARIS RESTAURANT'S VEAL OSKAR

11 to 12 ounces veal
  scallopine
salt and pepper to taste
flour
2 tablespoons butter

4 ounces backfin crabmeat
8 spears white asparagus
4 tablespoons Béarnaise
  sauce (mix or homemade)

Pound veal between waxed paper (or roll marble rolling pin over meat) until it is very thin. Salt and pepper both sides and lightly dredge in flour. Melt butter in a skillet and sauté veal until pure white. Put on 2 plates and top each portion with 2 ounces of crabmeat, 4 spears of asparagus, and dollops of Béarnaise sauce. Broil until lightly browned. Serves 2.

THE TREATY OF PARIS RESTAURANT'S EMPANADAS

¼ cup raisins
¼ cup brandy
2 tablespoons olive oil
1½ pounds beef tenderloin
  tips, diced
5 tablespoons tomato paste
½ to ¾ teaspoon crushed
  red pepper

½ teaspoon oregano
½ teaspoon basil
1 teaspoon salt
½ teaspoon pepper
1 to 2 eggs, well beaten
2 packages commercial puff
  pastry

Soak raisins in brandy until plump. In a skillet heat the olive oil. Sauté beef, then add raisins and all other ingredients except egg and pastry. Mix well. Roll puff pastry as directed, and cut into 48 3-inch rounds. On each of 24 rounds, place about 2 ounces of the meat mixture. Cover with the remaining rounds. Press edges of pastry together and brush with beaten egg to seal. Also brush tops with egg. Bake in a 325-degree oven for 25 to 30 minutes or until lightly browned. Yields 2 dozen.

THE PENWICK HOUSE
Dunkirk

THE PENWICK HOUSE

Want to know who is doing something about our national debt? The astute thinkers at The Penwick House. They discovered that the import of foreign wines accounts for approximately two per cent of the national debt. This fact, coupled with the belief that American vineyards are now producing some of the world's finest wines, inspired the Penwick House to develop an all-American wine list.

Having just glimpsed the Byrd Vineyards, nestled in the Catoctin Mountains, my daughter Daintry and I found our curiosity piqued. At the Penwick House, we satisfied that curiosity, sipping Byrd's 1981 Sauvignon Blanc as we looked out from a bay window onto an old-timey garden.

Often I am asked to explain this "romance" I pursue with the past. It's difficult to convey the exact type of romance offered by a restaurant in a fine old 1870 house. It has something to do with a garden with a gently curving walkway shaded by century-old trees . . . or wine served in an antique cut-glass carafe. Perhaps your ancestors lived in the manner of Dr. and Mrs. Chaney, who built the Penwick house. Perhaps, like me, you've read about this lifestyle and enjoy getting a taste of it. Whatever your background, it's fun to seek connections with the past.

While nibbling at a tasty Mushroom Turnover filled with subtly seasoned sour cream, we wondered what it must have been like to come here for a piano lesson when the home was owned by Miss Inez and her husband, Jimmy Jones, who ran his country store out back. We decided that Miss Inez couldn't have been as stern as her former pupils claim, as the front banister is still loose from heavy use by students.

A lovely, crunchy salad with a Honey and Lemon Juice House Dressing was accompanied by a basket of Hot Popovers, Sweet Cornbread and Bran Muffins so good that we almost considered not ordering entrées. But we knew that this was our last chance for Maryland seafood. I also knew that it was time for me to pare down calories, so I selected their Fresh Bass-Striped Rockfish. The fish was so tender and the sauce so flavorful that each bite seemed to melt in my mouth. My ninety-eight-pound daughter, who haughtily laughs at calories, not only devoured every bite of a creamy seafood entrée called Our Made Dish, but allowed me only one tiny bite of their custardy Amaretto Cheesecake.

The Penwick House is located on Route 4 in Dunkirk. Lunch is served from 11:30 a.m. until 2:00 p.m., Tuesday through Saturday. Dinner is served from 5:00 p.m. until 9:00 p.m., Tuesday through Thursday; from 5:00 p.m. until 10:00 p.m., Friday and Saturday; and from 4:00 p.m. until 8:00 p.m. on Sunday. Sunday brunch is from 10:30 a.m. until 2:30 p.m. For reservations (requested) call (301) 257-7077.

THE PENWICK HOUSE'S MUSHROOM TURNOVER

2 sticks softened butter
4 ounces softened cream
  cheese
2 cups all-purpose flour
1 pound fresh mushrooms,
  chopped
2 tablespoons additional
  butter

½ teaspoon thyme
½ teaspoon garlic salt
½ teaspoon white pepper
½ teaspoon oregano
½ tablespoon sour cream
1 beaten egg white

Mix butter and cream cheese together with wooden utensil. Add flour to mixture until completely incorporated. Cover bowl and refrigerate for 1 hour. Sauté mushrooms in additional butter until tender. Add thyme, garlic salt, white pepper and oregano. Remove from heat and add sour cream. Mix well and set aside. Remove dough from refrigerator and let stand for 45 minutes. Roll out dough into oval shapes. Fill half of each oval with mushroom mixture. Fold dough over and press sides together to seal. Brush egg white over sealed edges. Place turnovers onto a greased flat pan and bake in a preheated 350-degree oven for 15 to 25 minutes until golden brown. Serves 4 to 6.

THE PENWICK HOUSE'S AMARETTO CHEESECAKE

Crust:

1½ cups graham cracker crumbs

1 stick butter, melted
3 tablespoons sugar

Preheat oven to 425 degrees. Combine graham cracker crumbs, melted butter and sugar. Grease a 9-inch springform pan and press mixture into pan, coming ¾ of an inch up the sides. Bake about 5 minutes, remove from oven and let cool.

Filling:

1½ pounds softened cream cheese

1 cup sugar
3 eggs

½ cup melted butter
1 ounce Amaretto
1 cup whipped cream
1 pint fresh strawberries

In a mixing bowl beat cream cheese together with sugar until light and fluffy. Add eggs, one at a time, beating to incorporate after each addition. Blend in butter and Amaretto. Pour into cooled crust and bake at 350 degrees for 1¼ hours. Remove, cool to room temperature, and refrigerate for at least 12 hours. Carefully loosen pan and remove cake. Top with whipped cream and berries. Yields 1 cake.

BLAIR MANSION INN
Silver Spring

BLAIR MANSION INN

When I buy a wedding present it is usually china. Never would I dream of giving newlyweds a gift that would entitle them to vote. But in 1880, Abner Shoemaker gave his niece Abigail and her husband, Charles Newman, a piece of land that promised this opportunity. On the land was a grand colonial-style mansion designed by famed architect Stanford White. Straddling the boundary between Washington, D.C., and the state of Maryland, the new home entitled the young couple to national voting privileges, which at that time were not afforded to residents of the District of Columbia.

Unfortunately, the ne'er-do-well husband gambled Abigail's dream home away in a matter of years. The mansion, which bordered the land of the Blair family for whom Blair House in Washington was named, subsequently acquired its neighbor's name.

Through the years the mansion moved through many hands. It became a tea house, then a boarding house, and it is even rumored to have been a house of prostitution. During the late thirties the home was renovated and turned into a hotel by Esterlene Bell.

Standing in the foyer, Rebecca Schenck, my daughter Daintry and I listened to a 1910 Nickelodeon, which was America's first jukebox, and found it to be in terrific condition. The only difference is that it takes a dime to do what a nickel once did. I was also fascinated with the story surrounding a James & Bolmstorm piano that had resided in the White House until Harry S. Truman's first administration. It seems that Truman had had no luck trying to convince Congress to appropriate funds for White House repair until the leg of this piano crashed through the ceiling. Later, Mrs. Bell acquired the piano for her hotel.

As we lunched in the Library, we found that the stories were as bountiful and succulent as the food. Owner and chef Roger Zeender grew up in this family-operated restaurant, which is once again undergoing renovation. Much of the work will be structural, and I'm glad it won't disturb the

State Room, with its mural of the Maryland State Capitol and ceiling fresco map of colonial Washington.

Even though this house is steeped in history, Zeender's divine culinary ability is more contemporary. We enjoyed fabulous, freshly baked croissant appetizers stuffed with ham, cheese and a variety of vegetables, each offering its own unique flavor. We also tried wonderfully crisp, sweet, hot Pineapple Fritters that could easily be a dessert. For an entrée I chose their Crab Imperial, a fresh, light and delicately seasoned dish so different from the usual Crab Imperials that I've tasted that I asked for the recipe.

Becca and I decided that you never get too old for peanut butter, especially when it is joined with chocolate and honey and melted inside a croissant. While we ate the whole thing, Daintry enjoyed their homemade Strawberry Italian Ice.

This was our first restaurant in Maryland, and I'm afraid we broke the one-bite sampling rule by eating every delicious bite that was put in front of us. We're not one bit sorry.

Blair Mansion Inn is located at 7711 Eastern Avenue in Silver Spring. Lunch is served from 11:30 a.m. until 3:30 p.m., Monday through Friday. For reservations (recommended) call (301) 588-1688.

BLAIR MANSION INN'S CRAB IMPERIAL

1 pound lump backfin crabmeat	$1/8$ teaspoon Old Bay seasoning
1 egg yolk	$1/2$ teaspoon capers
$6^1/2$ tablespoons mayonnaise	3 egg whites

Pick shells from crabmeat. Add egg yolk, 2 tablespoons mayonnaise, Old Bay seasoning and capers and mix until well combined. With an electric mixer, beat egg whites until stiff; gently fold in $4^1/2$ tablespoons of mayonnaise and stir until mixed. Divide crabmeat mixture into 6 equal portions and place on a greased cookie sheet. Ladle egg white mixture evenly over tops of crabmeat and cook in a 375-degree oven for 10 minutes. Serves 6.

BLAIR MANSION INN'S CROISSANT-PEANUT MELT

2 tablespoons crunchy
  peanut butter
2 tablespoons clover honey

2 tablespoons chocolate
  chips
1 fresh bakery croissant

Combine peanut butter, honey and chocolate chips until well mixed. Split croissant almost in half and fill with mixture. Place croissant on a greased cookie sheet and bake at 350 degrees for 5 minutes. Serves 1.

BLAIR MANSION INN'S PINEAPPLE FRITTERS

3 eggs
1 cup milk
1 cup sugar
2 tablespoons vanilla
4 cups all-purpose flour
1½ tablespoons baking
  powder

1½ cups crushed pineapple,
  drained
1½ cups vegetable oil
1 cup powdered sugar

Combine first four ingredients and stir until mixture has a rough, wavy consistency. Add baking powder and drained pineapple and mix to incorporate. In a deep fryer, heat oil to 350 degrees. Drop well-rounded tablespoons of batter into hot oil. When fritters pop to surface, tap with spoon until they turn over to cook other side to a golden brown. Remove, drain on paper towel and keep warm until all batter is used. Roll fritters in powdered sugar. Yields about 40 fritters.

Note: Dip spoon in an extra bowl of vegetable oil after putting each fritter into deep fryer. This will help the next fritter slide easily from the spoon.

MRS. K'S TOLL HOUSE
Silver Spring

MRS. K'S TOLL HOUSE

Have you ever gone out to eat and filled up on bread before your meal arrived? This won't happen at Mrs. K's, explained Mr. K (which is short for Kreuzberg), because "we don't serve bread until after the first course. When friends ask how you liked the Country Fried Chicken or Pork Roast with Dressing, we want you to be able to tell them."

Taking those words to heart, we nibbled sparingly when a lazy susan chock-full of salad selections was set upon our table. Then we took a tour of this restaurant, which resembles an English country cottage complete with garden.

From the horse and buggy days of the 1900s until World War I, the restaurant building was a toll house, where travelers had to stop and pay a toll for the use and maintenance of the road. Later, the old toll house became a tea house, then a road house, where America's beloved Kate Smith once sang.

In 1931 the Kreuzbergs bought the road house and began serving "straight American food" amidst their antique collections. At Mrs. K's you'll see Staffordshire blue pottery, pressed glass plates that have been assembled into a plate glass window and an exquisite display of Nicholas Lutz glass. In the Dickens Lounge you'll fall in love with the "mouse" clock, fashioned after the nursery rhyme, "Hickory, Dickory, Dock." If arriving or departing at one o'clock, you'll see the mouse travel upward to one and fall down again.

We missed the mouse performance, but it was time for our meal, so we scurried back to our table in the garden room. Rebecca chose Baked Ham with Raisin Sauce. My one taste convinced me that the sauce was just sweet enough to enhance the moist, tender ham. I was lucky to get even a bite of Daintry's Old Fashioned Pot Roast as this "just right rare" roast is hard to come by anymore. Since I've tried Country Fried Chicken in every other state, I ordered the Maryland variety, and I wasn't disappointed. It was crisp without a heavy batter, and complemented by the surprise of Sherried Acorn Squash with a tart citrus flavor.

74

Though controlling ourselves was difficult, we let the bread accompany our meal instead of vice versa in order to have room for dessert. Their Slice Lemon Pie had a rich sweet and sour taste that I thought had gone out with my grandmother's baking. I was happy to find this elusive flavor—like so many secrets of old-fashioned culinary artistry—alive and well at Mrs. K's.

Mrs. K's Toll House is located at 9201 Colesville Road in Silver Spring. Lunch is served from 11:45 a.m. until 2:30 p.m., Tuesday through Saturday. Dinner is served from 5:00 p.m. until 8:30 p.m., Tuesday through Saturday. Sunday dinner is served from noon until 8:00 p.m. For reservations (recommended) call (301) 589-3500.

MRS. K'S TOLL HOUSE'S MACAROON PIE

3 egg whites	½ cup crushed pecans
1 cup sugar	12 crushed saltines
½ teaspoon baking powder	1 cup whipped cream

With an electric mixer beat egg whites until peaks begin to form. Combine sugar with baking powder and add to egg white mixture gradually, beating until stiff. Fold in pecans and saltines carefully until blended. Spoon into a greased 8- or 9-inch pie tin and bake in a 350-degree oven for 25 minutes. Cool. Serve with whipped cream. Yields 1 pie.

MRS. K'S TOLL HOUSE'S SLICE LEMON PIE

Pastry Crust:

3 cups plain flour	1 cup shortening
1 teaspoon salt	5 to 6 teaspoons ice water
2 teaspoons sugar	

Sift dry ingredients together, mixing until combined. Cube shortening and add to dry ingredients a few cubes at a time. With two knives or a pastry blender, cut the shortening into the dry ingredients until consistency is coarse and pebbly. Blend in 5 tablespoons ice water, one tablespoon at a time, pressing dough against bowl until it masses. Remove from bowl and divide in half. With heels of palms, press each half out to form a 4- to 5-inch circle. Add more ice water if dough breaks apart. Lightly flour each circle. Cover each with waxed paper and refrigerate from 20 to 60 minutes. Remove one circle from refrigerator, place on a floured board and roll out to fit into an 8-inch pie pan. Keep remaining dough chilled until ready to use.

Filling:

3 lemons, peeled	pinch of salt
4 medium eggs	1/2 cup water
2 1/2 cups sugar	dash of nutmeg
2 tablespoons melted butter	

Remove lemon cores and slice lemons very thin, removing seeds; set aside. In a mixing bowl, slightly beat the eggs before adding sugar, melted butter, salt, water and nutmeg. When well combined, stir in lemon slices. Pour mixture into pie crust. Roll out remaining crust and cover pie, pricking top for air vents. Bake in a 425-degree oven for 10 minutes, then reduce heat to 325 degrees and bake an additional 30 minutes. Yields 1 pie.

MRS. K'S TOLL HOUSE'S SHERRIED ACORN SQUASH

2 acorn squash	4 tablespoons dry sherry
salt to taste	2 tablespoons butter
4 tablespoons brown sugar	
2 teaspoons fresh grated orange peel	

Cut acorn squash in half and scoop out seeds. Sprinkle each half with salt. Place halves on a greased cookie sheet, with cut side down, in a 350-degree oven for 40 minutes. Turn cut side up and prick inside surface with a fork. Sprinkle each half with 1 tablespoon brown sugar, 1/2 teaspoon orange peel and 1 tablespoon sherry; dot each half with 1/2 tablespoon butter. Bake 10 minutes longer. Serves 4.

BROOK FARM INN OF MAGIC
Chevy Chase

BROOK FARM INN OF MAGIC

How would you like to find $40,000 in gold? During the Civil War, such a stash is rumored to have been brought to the grounds of the original house where the present Brook Farm Inn of Magic now stands. The house was used as a meeting place for Confederate spies, and Captain Mosby, known as the "Gray Ghost" of the Confederacy, supposedly brought the gold here one night in payment for the planned assassination of President Lincoln.

If found, the loot will represent the inn's greatest feat of magic, as all manner of devices have been used in unsuccessful searches for the gold. Actually, this unusual dinner theatre is better at levitating a volunteer lady from the audience than conjuring up that supposed stash. And levitation is only one trick out of their bag.

When I first heard the name, I thought that magic meant the enchantment of this rustic, charming structure located on Miss Minnehaha Brook's property. It isn't clear whether Miss Brook was named after the small Minnehaha Brook that cuts through the area, or the brook was later named after her. Customarily, Indian fathers named their babies after the first thing the father saw at the moment of the baby's birth.

At any rate, Minnehaha began the tradition of serving the public when she turned her log cabin into a tea room that served lunch. You can't get lunch anymore, but you can have continental cuisine served at your dinner table.

Realizing that energy was needed to keep up with this fast-paced evening, we ordered a Hat Trick appetizer of Portuguese Kale Soup. This very hearty and delicately spiced soup awakened our palates along with a substantial-bodied 1982 French Beaujolais.

It's always more fun when you are part of the act, so my mother's ring wound up on the stem of a wine glass that had to be broken to extricate the ring. This occurred in the midst of their tableside preparation of salad. It still boggles my mind.

Feats of magic are also performed in the kitchen. Rebecca

and Daintry made the Blackstone's Special, a tricky little chicken breast stuffed with a raisin and nut dressing, disappear along with the fresh Perch Provencale. Wanting something a little lighter, I chose The Grand Illusion, a Shrimp Louis salad embellished with tiny fresh bay shrimp, artichoke hearts, and many tasty et ceteras.

You needn't worry about picking up extra calories here as the magic tricks and high revelry will inspire enough laughter to burn up any calories over your daily limit.

Brook Farm Inn of Magic is located at 7101 Brookville Road in Chevy Chase. Dinner show seating is at 7:00 p.m. Wednesday and Thursday, 8:00 p.m. Friday. Saturday matinees for children are held every other Saturday at noon. Saturday dinner shows are at 5:00 p.m. and 9:00 p.m. Sunday dinner show is at 6:00 p.m. Close Up Theatre is performed from 7:30 p.m. until midnight weekdays, and to 1:00 a.m. on weekends. For reservations (required) call (301) 652-8820.

BROOK FARM INN OF MAGIC'S PORTUGUESE KALE SOUP

½ stick butter or margarine
½ pound diced prime rib or good quality beef
½ pound hot sausage
½ large onion, sliced thin
1 garlic clove, minced
2 quarts beef stock, commercial or homemade

1 15-ounce can kidney beans, drained
1 15-ounce can new potatoes, diced
1 15-ounce can peeled tomatoes, drained
6 ounces fresh kale
¼ pound cooked fettuccine

Melt butter or margarine in a Dutch oven or soup pot and add beef, sausage, onion and garlic. Sauté until sausage is done. Drain fat and add beef stock, kidney beans, new potatoes, tomatoes and kale. Reduce heat to medium and cook until kale is tender. Prepare fettuccine separately and add to soup a few minutes before serving. Yields about 3 quarts.

BROOK FARM INN OF MAGIC'S
BLACKSTONE'S SPECIAL

4 8-ounce chicken breasts
1 cup commercial stuffing
mix or 1 cup bread
crumbs

3 tablespoons melted butter
¼ cup boiling water
¼ cup crushed walnuts
¼ cup raisins

With a mallet, pound chicken breasts until thin and set aside. Mix stuffing or bread crumbs with melted butter and boiling water until combined. Add walnuts and raisins and mix until incorporated. Spoon stuffing mixture into center of chicken breasts and roll up. Secure with toothpicks. Place in a greased, shallow pan and bake in a 375-degree oven for 25 minutes.

Sauce:
½ cup white wine
1 shallot, chopped
¾ cup chicken stock
sprig of chopped fresh
tarragon or pinch of dried
tarragon

1 cup heavy cream
2 tablespoons butter
1 tablespoon flour
salt and pepper to taste

Place white wine and shallots in saucepan over high heat and cook until volume is reduced to ¼ of original amount. Add chicken stock and tarragon and reduce volume to ½. Add cream and reduce heat. In a separate saucepan make a roux by melting the butter and stirring in the flour until dissolved. Add roux to cream mixture, stirring to incorporate. Taste and add salt and pepper if desired. Pour sauce over cooked chicken and serve. Serves 4.

NORMANDIE FARM
Potomac

NORMANDIE FARM Its name is spelled differently now; it used to be Normandy Farms. A lounge is where the kitchen used to be, on the front of the house. And there are no petting farm animals down at the barn, which children used to admire when they visited the farm. But Normandie Farm is full of memories for the people of Potomac Village and Washington, and it's a matter of local pride to come back to the 1931 restaurant, "where the tradition of hot golden popovers and fine country cuisine continues."

When Gordon and I were at Normandie Farm for lunch, it was the bitter cold kind of day when schools are out and pipes are burst and camaraderie is strong. We found the great room, with a fire roaring at each end, nearly vacant, but a sizable group of people sat companionably close on a sun porch warmed by the sun and electric heaters.

Our table in front of the fire faced the Normandie coat of arms, a fleur-de-lis banner and copper pots hanging over the mantel. The French provincial room is full of folk art, from the rooster dishes displayed in cabinets to the sayings and songs inscribed on dark beams that stand out against stuccoed walls. We tried out the old French folk song "Alouette" as we sampled a house white wine, La Fleur. When the chef appeared with the most popped-over muffins I've ever seen, we sang to him. The Popovers, served with raspberry jam, were a wonderful appetizer to introduce the specialty of the house, Filet de Boeuf Wellington, served very pink and very tender. A layer of mushroom and pâté underneath puff pastry did not overpower the taste of tenderloin.

On the plate with the beef were two crisp potato balls, half a tomato breaded and broiled, and a small bundle of string beans "tied" with a strip of bacon. The three accompaniments were just right in color, taste and size. I liked the crispness of the beans and plan to adopt the cooking method myself, although I realize that some Southerners would call it treason to cook green beans for no more than five minutes.

When a jazz trio or a pianist entertains in the lounge, the music flows into the dining room through a door marked overhead with more folk song words: "Frère Jacques, dormez-vous?" A sign over another door, in the lounge decorated with 1930s prints, reads "Rick's Café American"—a place lots of us would still like to visit. But even if we never get to Paris, we'll always have the Normandie Farm.

Normandie Farm is located at 10710 Falls Road in Potomac. Lunch is served from 11:30 a.m. until 2:30 p.m., Tuesday through Saturday, and brunch from 11:00 a.m. until 2:30 p.m. on Sunday. Dinner is from 6:00 p.m. until 10:00 p.m., Tuesday through Thursday; from 6:00 p.m. until 11:00 p.m., Friday and Saturday; and from 5:00 p.m. until 9:00 p.m. on Sunday. For reservations (requested) call (301) 983-8838.

NORMANDIE FARM'S POPOVERS

8 eggs	1 teaspoon sugar
2 cups milk	3 cups all-purpose flour
1 teaspoon salt	12 teaspoons oil

Mix eggs, milk, salt and sugar. Add flour, and mix for 1 minute (do not overmix). Put 1 teaspoon of oil in each cup of a popover pan or muffin tin and preheat pan for 10 minutes. Then fill each cup ¾ full with batter. Bake for 15 minutes at 400 degrees. Reduce heat to 350 degrees, and bake for 30 more minutes or until done. Yields 12 large popovers (24 smaller popovers if muffin tins are used).

NORMANDIE FARM'S GREEN BEANS

24 whole string beans	salt
2 tablespoons butter	white pepper
2 shallots, chopped	1 tablespoon blanched almonds, sliced

Bring lightly salted water to a rapid boil, add beans and cook for 5 minutes. Remove beans, plunge them briefly into ice water, remove and set aside to drain. Melt butter in a skillet and lightly sauté beans with shallots. Add salt and white pepper to taste. Add almonds and mix lightly. Serve 6 to a plate as vegetable garnish (may be wrapped with slice of bacon or pimento). Serves 4.

Note: Beans may be boiled as directed by the pound and stored in refrigerator for future sautéing.

NORMANDIE FARM'S FILET DE BOEUF WELLINGTON

1 2½ pound beef
  tenderloin, whole,
  trimmed, peeled
2 ounces goose liver pâté
4 ounces fresh mushrooms,
  puréed in blender
¾ pound commercial puff
  pastry

1 egg
2 tablespoons water
4 ounces Madeira sauce
  (commercial)

Sear tenderloin on all sides, leaving the center practically raw. Cool. Spread with liver pâté and purée of mushroom. Roll out pastry ³/16 inch thick. Wrap pastry tightly around tenderloin, keeping seam on bottom. Fold ends under. Decorate with cut-outs made from pastry trimmings. Beat egg with water to make egg wash, and brush on surface of pastry. Place on a lightly oiled sheet pan. Bake in a 350-degree oven for 40 minutes or until pastry is done. If pastry browns too quickly, shield it with foil. Cut in slices about ¾ inch thick. Serve 1 slice per portion with Madeira sauce on the side. Serves 6.

OLD ANGLER'S INN
Potomac

OLD ANGLER'S INN I felt like an old angler myself, winding my way down the circular metal staircase from topside to the kitchen to question the chef about recipes. When I touched bottom, timers were ringing, oven doors being swung open and trays of food being rushed upstairs.

I knew the recipes would be worth the trouble, because the plate I had been served upstairs was a sight to behold. Sea scallops were surrounded by bits of vegetables—carrot, zucchini, broccoli, tomato, onion and cauliflower—and not-so-common morels, which are French mushrooms. The name of the dish is Le St. Jacques aux Morilles, or Sea Scallops with Morels and Cream Sauce. This entrée is typical of the French cuisine served at Old Angler's Inn.

The inn is proud of its age and prints "Since 1860" on its business cards as well as on the black menu folder, which also bears the image of a top-hatted "old angler" with a good-sized fish hooked to the end of his line.

The inn's location is historic, too, only fifteen minutes from the nation's capital and right across the road from the C&O Canal. Teddy Roosevelt fished here, and just think of the people (as well as the animals) who have walked the towpath beside the canal. Captain John Smith camped nearby in 1608 during a canoe trip up the Potomac (then spelled "Patauomeck") River, where Algonquin Indians had a post for traveling traders. George Washington designed the locks on the canal. And during the Civil War, men from both the North and South were guests at the inn.

Recently the canal towpath has attracted bikers and hikers, people interested in history and nature. In good weather they come to the Biergarten at Old Angler's Inn for food cooked outdoors and served on patio tables. But in winter it's the big stone fireplace in the downstairs lounge that draws friends together for drinks and conversation before they go upstairs to order dinner.

Gordon and I ate in a long room fitted to the pitch of the roof. The slanted ceiling was wallpapered almost to the top, where a strip of mirror ran from end to end. Murals painted on both long walls showed green canal scenes. We sipped the Muscadet house wine and imagined we were angling from a boat. Then up came Shrimp with Garlic Butter for Gordon, which complemented in looks and taste the Sea Scallops I had ordered.

Our prize catch for dessert was a bittersweet Chocolate Mousse made with a touch of rum (and more than a touch of whipped cream). I made the recipe at home in a single soufflé dish, but Old Angler's Mousse was swirled high in individual compotes. It took only one light, monogrammed wafer, stuck in the edge of each, to anchor the chocolate froth.

Old Angler's Inn is located at 10801 MacArthur Boulevard in Potomac. Lunch is served from noon until 3:00 p.m., Saturday and Sunday. Dinner is served from 6:00 p.m. until 10:30 p.m., Tuesday through Saturday, and from 5:00 p.m. until 9:30 p.m. on Sunday. For reservations (required) call (301) 365-2425.

OLD ANGLER'S INN'S SEA SCALLOPS
WITH MORELS AND CREAM SAUCE

8 dried morels (whole fresh
   mushrooms may be
   substituted)
³/₄ pound sea scallops
1 cup white wine

2 shallots, chopped
2 tablespoons dry, white
   vermouth
¹/₂ cup heavy cream

Soak dried morels in cold water to cover for 6 hours, changing water several times. Drain and pat dry. Cut scallops horizontally in slices of uniform thickness, and poach them in wine. Add shallots and vermouth, and cook over raised heat to reduce sauce until it thickens. Add cream and morels, and boil for about 1 minute. Serve immediately on a warm plate. Serves 2.

Note: This dish is enhanced by serving on each plate, with the scallops and morels, 1 or 2 pieces of lightly-blanched broccoli or cauliflower, zucchini or carrot. The vegetables, too, may be covered with sauce.

OLD ANGLER'S INN'S CHOCOLATE MOUSSE

6 ounces semisweet chocolate	4 egg yolks, beaten
1/3 cup rum	1 pint whipping cream
1 cup water	4 egg whites

Place chocolate, rum and water in the top of a double boiler. Heat over water until chocolate melts. Add beaten egg yolks to chocolate mixture and let cool to room temperature. Whip the cream and add it to the cooled chocolate. Whip egg whites into stiff peaks and carefully fold into mixture. Place in one bowl or in individual compotes, and refrigerate until ready to serve. Serves 8 to 10.

OLD ANGLER'S INN'S SHRIMP
SAUTEED WITH GARLIC BUTTER

2 tablespoons lightly salted butter	1/2 cup white wine
1 garlic clove, chopped	2 tablespoons heavy cream
12 jumbo shrimp	2 tablespoons sweet butter
	salt and pepper to taste

In a skillet melt salted butter, add garlic, and sauté shrimp until firm and white. Transfer shrimp to warm plates. Stir remaining ingredients into garlic butter residue until smooth. Raise heat to reduce sauce until it thickens. Pour sauce over the shrimp and serve immediately. Serves 2.

BRASS ELEPHANT
Baltimore

BRASS ELEPHANT

Have you ever watched a movie made in a foreign land and gotten so caught up in the mystery of an Indian temple, or some wonderful castle with carved marble fireplaces and crystal chandeliers, that afterward you were surprised to awake to reality? That is how we felt after lunch at the Brass Elephant. The interior dressings of this splendid old row house are a beautiful blend of Eastern and European styles of the eighteenth century. The restaurant owes its grandeur to two gentlemen: Charles Morton Stuart, who built the house, and second owner George Wroth Knapp, a gentleman trader who embellished the lavish setting with exotic sculptures of teak and brass from his Chinese and Indian trade routes.

Like a trio of visiting Indian princesses, Daintry, Rebecca and I passed beneath the subtly lighted brass elephant sconces on our way past the tapestried walls of the elegant downstairs dining room to lunch upstairs. Seated at a brass-trimmed, rosewood-inlaid table, we sipped their house wine, whose name translates to mean Fountains of the Pope. The wine is as enchanting as the room, which has stained glass windows and a carved marble elephant in the corner.

If the wine didn't clue you to the style of cuisine, the menu would. Chef Randall Stahl, graduate of the Culinary Institute of America, calls it Northern Italian with a French flair.

My daughter Daintry ordered the Veal Valdostano, which is topped with a creamy mushroom sauce and Fontina cheese. Daintry, who is becoming quite the connoisseur, remarked that Stahl cooks with a distinctive style. Rebecca, who had chosen the New York Sirloin Pizzaiola, agreed that her steak definitely had a highly original flavor.

We asked Stahl for his best dessert and were served his Chocolate Sabayon Cake. You've seen the expressions that menus use to describe desserts like this: decadent, sinful, voluptuous. All those descriptions fit this creation! Lingering over Cappuccino, we were reluctant to leave the leisurely life of that opulent yesteryear. But good movie dreams don't fade for me, especially when I can be part of the supporting cast.

Brass Elephant is located at 924 North Charles Street in Baltimore. Lunch is served from 11:30 a.m. until 2:00 p.m., Monday through Friday. Dinner is from 5:30 p.m. until 9:30 p.m., Monday through Thursday, from 5:30 p.m. until 11:00 p.m. on Friday and Saturday, and from 5:00 p.m. until 9:00 p.m. on Sunday. For reservations (recommended) call (301) 547-8480.

BRASS ELEPHANT'S CHOCOLATE SABAYON CAKE

8 large eggs, separated, at
  room temperature
$2/3$ cup sugar
$1/2$ teaspoon vanilla
1 scant cup soft cake flour
4 tablespoons cocoa powder

3 tablespoons cornstarch
$1^1/4$ teaspoons baking soda
3 tablespoons melted butter,
  cooled to room
  temperature
butter and sugar for pan

Beat egg yolks until thick and pale yellow. In a larger stainless steel or glass bowl, beat the egg whites on high speed, gradually adding sugar and vanilla; beat until stiff. Fold in beaten egg yolks with a rubber spatula. Mix with an electric mixer on lowest speed until doubled in volume. Sift together the flour, cocoa powder, cornstarch, and baking soda. Fold sifted ingredients into egg mixture a little at a time until well mixed. Add melted butter and mix until blended. Butter a 9-inch springform pan and sprinkle it with sugar. Fill $2/3$ full with batter. Bake in a 350-degree oven for 30-35 minutes or until cake tests done. Remove from pan and place on rack to cool.

Chocolate Sabayon Filling:
6 egg yolks
5 tablespoons sugar
$1/2$ cup cream sherry
1 teaspoon unflavored
  gelatin
5 ounces melted chocolate

$1^3/4$ cup heavy whipping
  cream
4 teaspoons confectioners'
  sugar
$1/4$ teaspoon vanilla
$1/8$ teaspoon almond extract

Combine egg yolks, sugar, sherry and gelatin in the top of a double boiler. Whip over hot water until thick and custard-like. Remove and whip until cool. Add melted chocolate to mixture. In a separate bowl whip heavy cream with confectioners' sugar, vanilla and almond extract until stiff, then blend chocolate-egg mixture with whipped cream mixture and refrigerate until thickened.

Simple Syrup:

1 cup sugar   **½ cup water**

Combine sugar and water in a small saucepan over medium-high heat. Stir constantly until sugar dissolves and mixture thickens to a syrup consistency. Remove from heat.

Slice cooled cake into 3 layers. Moisten layers with Simple Syrup and spread Chocolate Sabayon Filling between layers. Place cake in refrigerator until filling sets. Ice with chocolate-flavored whipped cream, and decorate with chocolate triangles or shaved chocolate. Yields one 9-inch cake.

BRASS ELEPHANT'S SHRIMP AND SCALLOPS MARINARA

8 large shrimp, peeled and deveined
½ pound sea scallops
2 garlic cloves, minced
2 teaspoons olive oil
3 ounces white wine
1 cup of Italian plum tomatoes
salt and pepper to taste

2 teaspoons basil
1 teaspoon oregano
½ teaspoon red pepper flakes
1 tablespoon chopped parsley
1 tablespoon butter
1 cup cooked linguine

Sauté shrimp and scallops with garlic in oil. Drain excess oil and add wine. Bring to a boil and add tomatoes, salt and pepper, basil, oregano, red pepper flakes and parsley. Simmer until seafood is cooked. Swirl butter into mixture and serve over linguine. Serves 2.

CHESAPEAKE RESTAURANT
Baltimore

CHESAPEAKE RESTAURANT

"**C**ut your steak with a fork or else tear up your check and walk out." That guarantee appeared in newspapers years ago when Chesapeake Restaurant first advertised Charcoal-Broiled Steaks. You know how tender they were, because the restaurant wasn't in business to lose money even when an à la carte steak cost eighty-five cents.

In the restaurant business, says Chesapeake owner Phil Friedman, even one new idea in twenty years isn't bad; but innovation is his family's specialty. Chesapeake claims to be the first restaurant east of the Rockies to serve Caesar Salad. In 1948 the Friedman brothers, Sidney and Philip, prepared it themselves tableside. They also were the first in Baltimore to serve a "New York" salad of mixed greens, adding Romaine and spinach to the customary lettuce leaves.

The menu reads in gold letters, "The Original Chesapeake, One of America's Best-Known Restaurants." The word "original" is stressed because the Chesapeake was closed briefly, and the owners want the public to know that it was reopened by the same people who started it in the first place. Chesapeake came into being in 1933 when Prohibition went out. But Chesapeake's place on the block had been established since 1918, when the father of the family opened a gourmet grocery among the brownstone townhouses.

The restaurant's cuisine is regional American, featuring seafood and prime beef. These two specialties are combined in the Crisfield Steak, a twelve-ounce sirloin strip stuffed with oysters. The dish takes its name from the birthplace of many a Maryland oyster, and I was glad to take the recipe home with me.

While we ate Armenian unleavened bread, we sampled the recommended house wine, an excellent Chateau Ducla that was halfway between dry and sweet. Then we watched our lunch being prepared tableside. Oysters Baltimore and Hot Spinach Salad . . . what a good combination. Plump oysters, lightly cooked in butter, sat atop a slice of pink prosciutto with toast points on either side.

Mr. Friedman assisted in tossing the salad ingredients, and I could picture him preparing Caesar Salads years ago. He has a deft hand as well as a smooth tongue. A bit of the latter seems to have passed on to the next generation. As a son in the business hurried by our table, he hailed us with an apologetic, "Nice to have *not* met you."

Chesapeake Restaurant is located at 1701 North Charles Street in Baltimore. Meals are served from 11:30 a.m. until 11:00 p.m., Sunday through Friday, and from 5:00 p.m. until midnight on Saturday. For reservations (recommended) call (301) 837-7711.

CHESAPEAKE RESTAURANT'S OYSTERS BALTIMORE

¹/₄ pound butter	4 thin slices prosciutto,
1 pint select oysters	Smithfield or smoked
freshly ground pepper	ham
	4 slices bread

In a skillet, melt butter, add oysters and fresh ground pepper to taste, and cook oysters until heated through. Meanwhile, heat sliced ham in oven or under broiler. Toast bread and cut in half diagonally for toast points. Place ham on heated serving plate with a toast point on either side. Spoon oysters (with some butter) over ham. Serves 4.

Note: This can be prepared tableside in a chafing dish or skillet. A variation of the method is to julienne the ham and sauté it along with the oysters.

CHESAPEAKE RESTAURANT'S HOT SPINACH SALAD

¹/₂ pound fresh spinach	12 croutons
3 strips bacon, cooked and chopped	2 fresh mushrooms, thinly sliced
2 ounces toasted pine nuts	1 hard boiled egg, chopped
3 ounces Vinaigrette Dressing (recipe below)	freshly ground black pepper

95

Remove stems from spinach; thoroughly wash and drain the leaves. Pat dry with a clean towel. In a skillet thoroughly heat the cooked, chopped bacon. Add pine nuts and Vinaigrette Dressing, and bring to a sizzle. In the meantime, place spinach in salad bowl and add croutons, mushrooms and egg. When dressing is hot, pour it over the spinach mixture. Add pepper to suit your taste. Toss lightly and serve immediately. Serves 2.

Vinaigrette Dressing:

1/2 teaspoon salt	1 tablespoon pimento,
1/2 cup wine vinegar	chopped
1 1/2 cups oil	1/2 teaspoon garlic
1/4 medium onion, chopped	1/4 teaspoon white pepper
1 shallot, chopped	

Combine all ingredients and mix thoroughly. Yields 1 pint.

CHESAPEAKE RESTAURANT'S CRISFIELD STEAK

6 to 8 raw oysters, with	4 ounces Bordelaise sauce
natural juices	(commercial or
2 12-ounce sirloin strip	homemade)
steaks	1 ounce brandy (optional)

Very lightly poach oysters in their own juices. Reserve oyster liquid. Cut pockets in steaks from front end. Stuff pockets with 3 to 4 oysters. Using either thin cord or small skewers, seal ends of steaks to hold in oysters. Broil steaks to desired doneness. While steak is broiling, heat Bordelaise sauce and combine with about an ounce of reserved oyster liquid. Place steak on preheated plate. If desired, add brandy to sauce and ignite. Pour sauce over steak and serve immediately. Serves 2.

Note: For "showing off," brandy can be flamed tableside.

HAUSSNER'S RESTAURANT, INC.
Baltimore

HAUSSNER'S RESTAURANT, INC.

"**I** hear from twenty reliable witnesses that you have married a most charming lady," H. L. Mencken wrote to William H. Haussner in 1935. Fifty years later, Maryland restaurateurs agree that Mrs. Frances Haussner is still a most charming lady. She presides over the restaurant her late husband established in 1926. The restaurant began in a building across the street and then expanded to incorporate five dwellings on Eastern Avenue.

Gordon and I have often stopped in Baltimore just to enjoy a meal at Haussner's. I always take home a few postcards showing paintings from the Haussner art collection, which shares the stage with the food.

"Masterpieces in art and dining" is the subheading on the menu and the postcards. Paintings that Mrs. Haussner bought at private auctions and estate sales cover almost every inch of wall space.

The museum-like second floor holds more art, including sections of the Pantheon de la Guerre, a life-sized painting of six thousand heroes from World War I. The Haussners salvaged the painting, and tried to find a home for it. No one place was able to handle the 45-foot by 402-foot work; however, a reconstructed portion is permanently mounted on a wall of the Liberty Memorial in Kansas City.

Then there is that other masterpiece: the dining. Looking at a list of thirty-five vegetables on the menu and not being able to narrow my favorites to fewer than five, I ordered a vegetable plate. My choices were Creamed Spinach (a specialty at Haussner's), Stewed Tomatoes, Candied Sweet Potatoes, Cauliflower and Fried Eggplant. On other visits I have selected from among their fine German entrées. This time I obtained the recipe for one of my favorites, Sauerbraten, because to follow Haussner's recipe is to follow the leader. Just preparing the marinade of vinegar, Burgundy, lemon halves and cinnamon sticks is a sensory experience.

The most popular dessert at Haussner's is Strawberry Pie, which is displayed with other delectable pastries in a take-out bakery department.

What do they call their cuisine besides German? The Haussners' daughter says, "Mother calls it healthy."

Haussner's Restaurant, Inc., is located at 3244 Eastern Avenue in Baltimore. Meals are served from 11:00 a.m. until 11:00 p.m., Tuesday through Saturday. Reservations are not accepted for dinner. For group reservations for lunch call (301) 327-8365.

HAUSSNER'S RESTAURANT, INC.'S STRAWBERRY PIE

1½ cups sugar
½ teaspoon strawberry
 flavoring
½ teaspoon red food
 coloring
1½ cups boiling water
3 tablespoons cornstarch
 dissolved in ½ cup water
1 cup Pastry Cream (recipe
 below)

1 prebaked deep 9-inch pie
 shell
1½ pints fresh strawberries,
 washed and hulled (keep
 whole if small; cut in
 half lengthwise if large)
whipped cream for
 decorating
¼ cup toasted slivered
 almonds

To make a glaze, add sugar, strawberry flavoring and food coloring to boiling water. Add dissolved cornstarch and stir over medium-high heat until mixture thickens. Remove from stove and set aside. Prepare Pastry Cream and let it cool, then spread in bottom of baked pie shell. Pour in ½ pint of strawberries, cover with half the water-sugar glaze and add remaining strawberries. Cover with remaining glaze. Decorate the edge with a circle of whipped cream and sprinkle with slivered almonds. Chill and serve. Yields 1 large pie.

Pastry Cream:
1 cup milk
3 egg yolks
¼ cup plus 2 tablespoons
 sugar

¼ cup all-purpose flour
1½ teaspoons vanilla
1 to 1½ tablespoons butter,
 softened

Scald milk in a saucepan and set it aside. In a bowl, whisk together the egg yolks and sugar until light in color and very thick, then beat in the flour. Pour the warm milk slowly into egg mixture and blend well. Pour mixture into saucepan and cook, stirring with a whisk, over low heat until mixture comes to a boil. It will appear lumpy at first; keep whisking. Make sure mixture does not stick to bottom of pan and burn.

Remove from heat. Add vanilla and butter. Cover surface with buttered waxed paper so it does not form a skin. Allow to cool.

HAUSSNER'S RESTAURANT, INC.'S SAUERBRATEN

3½ cups Burgundy
1 quart vinegar
2½ cups sugar
12 lemons, halved and
    squeezed, juice reserved
1 pound onions, chopped
½ cup mixed pickling spice
2 sticks whole cinnamon
4 pounds top sirloin butt
flour
1 teaspoon salt
½ teaspoon seasoning salt
½ pound gingersnap
    cookies, crushed
2 bay leaves

In a glass or ceramic bowl (do not use metal), mix together 3 cups Burgundy, the vinegar, 2 cups sugar, reserved lemon juice, lemon halves, onions, pickling spice and cinnamon. Add meat and let it marinate in a cool place for a few days. Be sure the marinade completely covers the meat.

Remove the meat and place it in a roasting pan with about 4 cups of marinade. Roast in a 350-degree oven for 2 to 3 hours or until done. Remove meat to a platter and keep warm. Skim off extra fat from pan and place it in a saucepan. Add enough flour to make a smooth roux. Cook over low heat for 3 to 4 minutes.

Into the roux strain pan juices and reserved marinade that was not cooked with meat. Add remaining ½ cup Burgundy, ½ cup sugar, salt, seasoning salt, gingersnaps and bay leaves. Whisk together as mixture comes to a boil. Lower heat and simmer for about 20 minutes. If this gravy is too thick, add water; if too thin, simmer a little longer to reduce. Slice meat and place on individual plates. Pour gravy over and serve. Serves 8.

100

SABATINO'S
Baltimore

SABATINO'S

Early photographs of Little Italy in Baltimore City show a distinctive feature at the intersection of Fawn and High Streets: a single post that appears to hold up the corner of a building. That building was the neighborhood candy store, which changed names as it changed owners—Granese's, Lou's or Corky's. Residents of the neighborhood point to the supporting post in pictures and say they remember it from childhood. At some time of modernization the column was enclosed, but it was exposed again when the building became Sabatino's in 1955.

Row houses are practically synonymous with Baltimore, and Sabatino's is made up of three of them. The restaurant preserves the integrity of the neighborhood by keeping the three exteriors separate in colors and materials as well as stoops and chimneys. Interiors, too, retain arched openings to show former divisions, so a diner knows whether he's sitting in the second or third house or in the former confectionery itself, where the restaurant first opened.

My favorite room is upstairs in the "house" furthest from the corner, where black and white photographs of relatives, friends and former neighbors hang on the walls. The photo gallery makes an impressive memorial.

Rick Rotondo, whose grandfather is one of those pictured upstairs, spoke respectfully of the restaurant's founders, Joseph Canzani and Sabatino Lupereni. Rick is one of the present owners and says he knows ninety percent of the people who come to Sabatino's. He began meeting them when he was sixteen and became a front man (while his brother became a chef). Celebrity customers include Frank Sinatra, Liberace and Anthony Quinn, who came seven times during a two-week theater production of Zorba the Greek.

We enjoyed the house red wine, Marca Petri Pastoso. In a way I'm sorry I tasted the Garlic Bread, an appetizer, because now I know what I missed by not getting the recipe. It is being marketed in stores, as is Sabatino's House Dressing. I can only say the mixture of garlic butter with oregano, red pepper, basil and cheese is special.

102

The sauces on our entrées were very different even though both contained sherry, lemon juice and chicken broth. Gordon's Shrimp Scampi featured jumbo shrimp in a sauce that was spicy with garlic and other seasonings. My Veal Francese's coating of egg batter and crumbs turned its sherry-flavored sauce a beautiful brown. Gordon and I divided the food; it was too good not to share.

I wanted a good, simple spaghetti sauce recipe from Little Italy, and I got it in Sabatino's Marinara. Haven't I heard that some people eat spaghetti for breakfast? I might return to Sabatino's to try that. They're open till 3:00 a.m.

Sabatino's is located at 901 Fawn Street in Baltimore. Meals are served from 11:30 a.m. until 3:00 a.m., daily. For reservations (recommended; required on weekends) call (301) 727-9414.

SABATINO'S VEAL FRANCESE A LA SABATINO

2 eggs, beaten
pinch of fresh parsley
pinch of salt
pinch of pepper
1/2 cup half and half
1 1/2 cups bread crumbs (or
   more)
1 to 1 1/4 pounds veal
   scallopine

3 tablespoons butter
4 tablespoons oil
2 tablespoons flour
3/4 cup sherry
juice of 1/4 lemon
3/4 cup chicken broth
4 slices lemon

Combine eggs, parsley, salt, pepper and half and half to make batter. Place bread crumbs in a separate bowl. Pound each slice of veal thin between layers of waxed paper. Dip in egg batter, then coat both sides with bread crumbs, shaking off loose breading. In a heavy skillet, heat butter with oil, and fry coated veal until it is golden brown. Remove veal and set aside on warm platter. Add flour to pan and stir until brown. Add sherry and lemon juice, then chicken broth. Simmer for 3 minutes. Pour over fried veal and garnish with lemon slices. Serves 4.

SABATINO'S SPAGHETTI AND MARINARA SAUCE

2 teaspoons crushed fresh
  garlic
4 tablespoons oil
4 cups whole peeled
  tomatoes
2 teaspoons oregano
1 teaspoon basil
1 teaspoon crushed red
  pepper

2 teaspoons chopped fresh
  parsley
1 teaspoon monosodium
  glutamate (optional)
1/2 teaspoon salt
8 ounces spaghetti

In a large saucepan or heavy skillet fry garlic in oil until golden brown. Add tomatoes and spices, and simmer over low heat for 20 minutes. Serve over spaghetti cooked according to package directions. Serves 4.

SABATINO'S SHRIMP SCAMPI

4 tablespoons oil
3 tablespoons butter
2 teaspoons crushed fresh
  garlic
20 jumbo shrimp
1/2 teaspoon crushed red
  pepper
1 teaspoon oregano

1/2 teaspoon salt
1/2 teaspoon monosodium
  glutamate (optional)
2 tablespoons flour
1/2 cup sherry
juice of 1/4 lemon
3/4 cup chicken broth

In a heavy skillet, heat oil and butter; add garlic and sauté until slightly brown. Add shrimp and cook until firm. Add spices and flour, stirring well. Add sherry and lemon juice, then chicken broth. Simmer over low heat for 10 minutes. Place 5 shrimp on each of 4 plates and cover with sauce. Serves 4.

SOCIETY HILL BAR, RESTAURANT
AND HOTEL
Baltimore

SOCIETY HILL

Having enjoyed a stay at Philadelphia's Society Hill Bar, Restaurant and Hotel while researching a book on Pennsylvania's historic restaurants, I couldn't wait to visit its counterpart in Baltimore. I was so eager, in fact, that I was their first guest on opening day.

The residence-turned-hotel is found in the center of the Mount Vernon district. This district was Baltimore's most fashionable residential area from early to mid-nineteenth century. The land was once the "Belvedere" estate of Colonel John Eager Howard, a Revolutionary War patriot and statesman. The nearby Washington Monument was erected on land that he donated to the city, and his philanthropic heirs gave the balance of land for use as public parks.

The restaurant is located on the basement level of the hotel. The main dining room is appointed with handsome tapestry-like floral banquettes and three tiny recessed windows that give the room a subdued, intimate feeling. Around the corner you'll find a sophisticated jazz piano bar. But my hands-down favorite dining area is an atrium with a semicircular glass ceiling, a white brick wall and large green trees. The sleek, contemporary atmosphere of this room was unexpected after a regal night in the turn-of-the-century hotel, where the bedrooms are lavishly furnished with beautifully coordinated antiques.

In our hotel room, Rebecca, Daintry and I had awakened to freshly squeezed orange juice, wonderful homemade Coffee Cake and fresh flowers on our breakfast trays. In the dining room for lunch, we received the same pampering.

Both the Italian Hot Pot and the California Connection had been recommended, so I decided to give both a sample—for the sake of our readers, of course. The Hot Pot was an original and exciting combination that could have belonged to none other than succulent, spicy Italian cuisine. The delicious California Connection, which I enjoyed with a dry red wine, was what I had come to expect from Society Hill kitchens. They delight in serving the latest creations in the lap of their luxurious antique settings.

Society Hill Bar, Restaurant and Hotel is located at 58 West Biddle Street in Baltimore. Lunch is served from 11:30 a.m. until 3:00 p.m., Monday through Friday. Dinner is served daily from 5:00 p.m. until 10:00 p.m. Brunch is served from 11:30 a.m. until 3:00 p.m. on Saturday, and from 11:00 a.m. until 2:30 p.m. on Sunday. Reservations are unnecessary, but the telephone number is (301) 837-3630.

SOCIETY HILL BAR, RESTAURANT AND HOTEL'S COFFEE CAKE

2¼ cups all-purpose flour
¾ cup sugar
1 cup light brown sugar
¾ cup vegetable oil
1¾ teaspoons cinnamon

½ cup chopped pecans
1 egg
1 teaspoon baking powder
1 teaspoon baking soda
1 cup buttermilk

Mix flour, both sugars, vegetable oil and ½ teaspoon of cinnamon together with electric mixer until mixture becomes coarse and pebbly. Remove ¾ cup and reserve for topping. Add remaining cinnamon and pecans, mixing until combined. In a separate bowl, combine egg, baking powder, baking soda and buttermilk, and add to first mixture. Pour mixture into a greased 9x12-inch pan and sprinkle with topping mixture. Pat topping lightly into place. Bake in a 350-degree oven for 30 minutes or until cake tester comes out clean. Yields 1 coffee cake.

SOCIETY HILL BAR, RESTAURANT AND HOTEL'S ITALIAN HOT POT

Sausage Stock:
2 tablespoons vegetable oil
1 pound hot Italian sausage
1½ cups coarsely chopped
  mushrooms
2 cups sliced onions
1 28-ounce can peeled
  tomatoes, undrained
1 6-ounce can tomato purée

1¼ cups dry white wine
1 cup clam juice
2 tablespoons fresh basil,
  chopped, or 1 tablespoon
  dried basil, crumbled
1 heaping tablespoon
  minced garlic

In a Dutch oven heat oil; add sausage, mushrooms and onions, breaking up sausage while stirring over medium heat. Cook until sausage loses pink color. Stir in tomatoes with juice, crushing tomatoes into small pieces. Reduce heat to low and simmer for 10 minutes. Pour in tomato purée, wine and clam juice and return mixture to a boil. Reduce heat to low, cover and simmer 30 minutes, stirring occasionally. Add basil and garlic and cook for 15 minutes more.

**Sausage Stock (recipe
 above)
4 tablespoons chopped fresh
 parsley**

**24 clams in shells
chopped fresh parsley for
 garnish
French bread**

Bring Sausage Stock to a boil. Stir in parsley and clams. Cover, reduce heat to medium and simmer about 5 minutes or until clams open. Remove clams from shells. Ladle Sausage Stock into 4 individual soufflé dishes, placing 6 clams (without shells) in each dish. Place under broiler for 1 minute. Sprinkle with additional parsley and serve with French bread. Serves 6 or more.

SOCIETY HILL BAR, RESTAURANT AND HOTEL'S CALIFORNIA CONNECTION

**4 flour tortillas
1 pound sliced roast beef
4 slices of large onion
12 slices of tomato
1 cup shredded lettuce**

**½ cup alfalfa sprouts (or
 less)
horseradish sauce
 (commercial)**

Down the center of each tortilla, lay 4 ounces roast beef, 1 onion slice, 3 tomato slices, one-fourth of shredded lettuce and one-fourth of alfalfa sprouts. Fold one side of tortilla over the other and secure with a toothpick. Place tortillas on a baking sheet in a 300-degree oven. Cook until hot but not dried out, about 2 to 3 minutes. Serve horseradish sauce on the side. Serves 4.

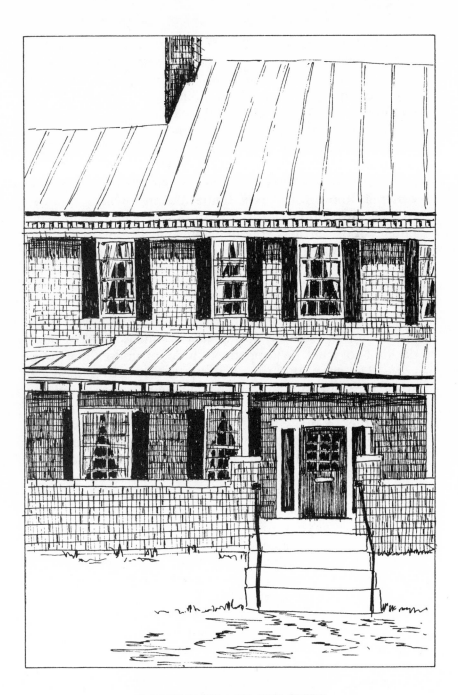

COUNTRY FARE INN
Owings Mills

COUNTRY FARE INN

How would you like to grow up having the job of a "lookout" for Indians? Apparently that was the job of millionaire Samuel Owings' children in this 1767 Federal-style mansion. The space where a window was inserted in the chimney is only large enough for a child. It sounds like a dull job, but the guard could be changed often because Owings had twelve children.

When modern families outgrow their surroundings, they generally move to a larger home, but in Owings' day new rooms were added with the birth of each child. Many such houses took on a crazy-quilt appearance, but in Owings' "U.L.M." house (named with the initials of the upper, lower and middle mills of the Owings empire), the only evidence of enlargement is the soft texture of interior brick walls that never weathered the elements.

Because this restaurant blooms with springtime pastels, our thoughts were on spring, and Daintry, Rebecca and I decided to whet our appetites outdoors under their grape arbor. However, the arrival of subtle Smoked Salmon and spicy Escargot Moutarde coincided with a high wind that sent us back inside, where anchoring was unneeded.

A "little" soup with big quality is their Petite Marmite, which gave one of my favorites, their Cream of Broccoli, a lot of competition. Then, to cleanse our palates, we sampled three Sorbets. My sweet tooth voted for the Strawberry.

Wisdom told us that sample bites of the wonderfully varied entrées should suffice, but that was before the first taste. I dare anyone to hold to one bite at this restaurant. Mignonette of Beef Forestière, Shrimp Moutarde in a delicate cream sauce and L'Escalope de Veau aux Champignons all tied for blue ribbons with Le Canard Roti au Poivre Vert, duck in a green peppercorn sauce.

The reason we originally intended just to sample the entrées was that we had seen the pastry cart showing off at neighboring tables. Among my many weak spots, home-made pastry is the weakest. September 7th Cake proved sensational, as did their Chocolate Lovers Cake.

Since Classical French cooking is not synonymous with low-calorie dining, Country Fare Inn includes the option of Nouvelle Cuisine. For those like me, who refuse to deny themselves the joy of an elegant restaurant during times when the belt rebels, this option is a delicious solution.

Country Fare Inn is located at 100 Painters Mill Road in Owings Mills. Lunch is served from 11:30 a.m. until 2:00 p.m., Monday through Friday. Dinner is served from 5:30 p.m. until 9:30 p.m., Monday through Thursday; from 5:30 p.m. until 10:00 p.m., Friday and Saturday; and from 4:00 p.m. until 9:00 p.m. on Sunday. For reservations (recommended) call (301) 363-3131.

COUNTRY FARE INN'S STRAWBERRY SORBET

1 quart fresh strawberries, puréed	½ cup water
	½ cup strawberry liqueur
14 to 16 ounces sugar	juice of 1 lemon
½ cup corn syrup	

Combine all ingredients in a bowl, mixing until thoroughly incorporated. Taste, and add more sugar if strawberries are not sweet enough. Place mixture in an ice cream freezer and freeze according to freezer directions. After freezing, sorbet should be semi-soft. Place in a plastic container with tight-fitting lid and store in the freezer. Yields over 2 quarts.

COUNTRY FARE INN'S LE CANARD
ROTI AU POIVRE VERT

1 4- to 5-pound duck	⅓ cup beef stock or 1 teaspoon bouvril
2 tablespoons green peppercorns	1 tablespoon dry vermouth
1 to 2 cups water	⅓ cup chicken stock
2 tablespoons butter	1 cup heavy cream
¼ cup brandy	salt and pepper to taste
1 tablespoon flour	cooked wild rice

111

Roast duck about 1 hour at 450 to 500 degrees, basting with duck grease drippings 3 times. Cool duck; cut in two and remove breast bones, rib bones and leg bones. Finish cooking duck halves at 325 to 350 degrees for about 20 minutes in a roasting pan with just enough water to prevent sticking. Do not overcook. To make sauce, rinse green peppercorns in water and drain. In a skillet melt butter and sauté peppercorns for 1 to 2 minutes. Add brandy and ignite. Shake pan until alcohol burns off; set aside. In a separate skillet combine flour and beef stock or bouvril. Stir into a paste over medium heat. Add vermouth and chicken stock and let mixture come to a boil, stirring constantly. Reduce volume to half and stir into green peppercorn mixture. Add heavy cream, salt and pepper, whisking to incorporate. Reduce slightly. Slice duck and serve over cooked wild rice with sauce ladled over top. Serves 4 or more.

COUNTRY FARE INN'S ESCARGOT AU MOUTARDE

8 large escargots	**2 shallots, chopped**
2 tablespoons butter	**¼ cup brandy**

Rinse escargots in cold water and drain. Put 2 tablespoons butter in a skillet and sauté shallots and escargots for 2 to 3 minutes. Add brandy and ignite. Shake pan until flame is extinguished and set aside, keeping warm.

Moutarde Sauce:

2 tablespoons butter	**3 teaspoons Pommery**
2 tablespoons flour	**mustard**
1 cup hot beef stock	**salt and white pepper**
1 teaspoon sweet vermouth	**4 tablespoons heavy cream**
1 teaspoon Dijon mustard	**4 baked pastry shells**

In a skillet, melt butter over medium heat and add flour; stir into a paste. Add beef stock and vermouth and whisk until smooth. Stir in both mustards until thoroughly mixed. Add salt and white pepper to taste, whisking for 1 minute. Add cream and whisk until flavors develop. Remove doughy centers from hot pastry shells and put 2 escargots inside each pastry shell; ladle sauce over top. Serves 4.

FIORI
Reisterstown

FIORI

Since Fiori means "flower" in Italian, it's appropriate for this restaurant serving Italian cuisine to have a garden out back. In a 100- by 50-foot plot, they grow not only flowers for their tables, but also fruits, vegetables and herbs. Cherries from the trees take the place of after-dinner mints—a classy touch—and there is plenty of basil for pasta. In pleasant weather, the host invites guests to walk around the garden after their meal.

The 1723 building has always been a public institution—whether a toll station or stagecoach stop on the Westminster Pike, a restaurant, or a hotel—but it resembles a comfortable home. When Gordon and I parked in front of it on a snowy night, we were warmed even before we entered by a glimpse, through the windows, of a bright fire at the end of a pine-paneled room. It was our first visit to Fiori, but ninety percent of the clientele returns, and I hope we will too.

For an appetizer, we divided a plate of Hot Antipasto so we could sample several different things—among them Homemade Sausage, Stuffed Eggplant and Mussels Marinara (which Fiori taught me to make). We also shared an order of Spinach Pie, a flaky pastry filled with spinach and Ricotta cheese. Served here as either appetizer or side dish, it could be lunch for me.

Gordon ordered Chicken Valdostano and enjoyed the sauce that was served over the chicken breast. I liked the presentation of the dish, with wild rice on one side, sprinkled with almonds, and a row of snow peas on the other.

After so many good appetizers, I was primed for Fettuccine Primavera, a really warming dish with creamy noodles and Romano cheese. The good broccoli and zucchini surrounding the pasta made me wish I had a vegetable garden.

Sometimes the restaurant makes vegetable-tinted pasta—spinach green, plain egg for white, and beet or tomato red—to create the colors of the Italian flag. On occasion they even dye coconut to make green, white and red Cannoli. I would have ordered the Italian dessert, but I didn't have room for Cannoli of any color.

Fiori is located at 808 Westminster Road in Reisterstown. Lunch is served from 11:30 a.m. until 2:30 p.m. on Friday only. Dinner is served from 5:00 p.m. until 9:00 p.m., Monday through Thursday; from 5:00 p.m. until 10:00 p.m., Friday and Saturday; and from 4:00 p.m. until 8:30 p.m. on Sunday. For reservations (recommended) call (301) 833-6300.

FIORI'S FETTUCCINE PRIMAVERA

12 ounces fettuccine
2 cups heavy cream
2 egg yolks
4 tablespoons butter
salt and pepper to taste
1/4 teaspoon oregano

1 teaspoon chopped fresh
  parsley
8 ounces Romano cheese,
  freshly grated
8 slices zucchini
8 broccoli florets

Bring 2 quarts of salted water to a boil. Add fettuccine and cook until al dente (firm to the bite). Remove fettuccine from water and rinse to wash off starch; set aside. In a separate pan over medium heat combine cream and egg yolks, stirring constantly. Add butter, salt, pepper, oregano, parsley and cheese. Let simmer over medium heat, still stirring. Add fettuccine to this sauce and toss to coat the noodles. Remove fettuccine and distribute it on 4 plates. Place two pieces of each vegetable at edge of each plate. Reduce the remaining sauce over increased heat to medium thickness. Pour sauce over pasta and serve. Serves 4.

Note: Other vegetables, such as snow peas, asparagus or cauliflower, may be substituted or added.

FIORI'S MUSSELS MARINARA

Sauce:
4 garlic cloves
1/4 medium onion, sliced
  thin
4 tablespoons olive oil
3 cups Italian plum
  tomatoes, peeled

1/2 cup white wine
salt and pepper to taste
1/8 teaspoon basil
1/8 teaspoon marjoram
1/4 teaspoon oregano
2 hot pepper flakes

115

Peel skin off garlic and smash cloves. Sauté with onion in olive oil until brown. Add tomatoes, wine and spices. Simmer and skim off foam to remove acid. Adjust seasoning.

½ cup butter
2 garlic cloves
40 medium mussels,
   cleaned

1 cup white wine
Italian bread

In large skillet, heat butter, braise garlic and add mussels and white wine. Steam for 2 to 3 minutes, until mussels open. Add sauce and adjust seasoning. Remove mussels to a platter. Reduce sauce over increased heat. Pour sauce over open mussels. Serve with Italian bread. Yields about 5 appetizer servings.

FIORI'S SPINACH PIE

1 pound fresh spinach
1 tablespoon salt
1 tablespoon butter
¼ cup chopped onion
3 eggs, beaten
12 ounces Ricotta cheese

4 ounces Provolone cheese,
   grated
¼ pound fillo dough
   (commercial), thawed
½ cup melted butter

Wash spinach until no sand remains. Place it in a bowl with 1 tablespoon of salt and cover with water. After spinach wilts, remove it from water, drain and chop it. In a skillet, melt 1 tablespoon butter and sauté onion; let cool. Combine onion with eggs and cheeses, and mix thoroughly with the spinach. Cut and roll fillo dough to fit four individual casseroles, 12 layers for each serving. Brushing each layer of dough with melted butter, lay 6 layers on the bottom of each casserole. Fill with one-fourth the amount of spinach mixture, and top with 6 more layers of buttered dough. Bake in a 350-degree oven for 15 minutes or until pastry is golden brown. Serves 4.

MILTON INN
Sparks

MILTON INN

Would you have turned Clark Gable from your door, even if he was with Carole Lombard? Neither would I, but that was the actor's reception at the Milton Inn when it was the private home of Polly Leiter. According to the story, the Gables were so intrigued by Maryland's antiques that one of Leiter's friends assured Hollywood's golden couple that they would be welcome at Leiter's antique-filled home. Unfortunately, no one told Polly Leiter, who had instructed her butler to admit no callers while she was taking a nap to relieve a champagne hangover. Bad timing, what?

Our timing was much better—we arrived just before lunch. In another month we might have dined on the garden patio surrounded by lillies-of-the-valley, azaleas and giant shade trees that may be as old as the 1740 fieldstone dwelling. The side entrance led us through the bar and into the cocktail lounge, which was the kitchen in the house's early days. Hot meals were prepared at the room's fireplace for the coachmen who drove Quakers down the road to monthly religious services at the New Gunpowder Meeting House. The residence, which is the oldest standing building in Baltimore county, is thought to have been built by a Quaker named Thom.

After its use as a coachmen's inn, the ivy-covered structure was transformed in 1847 into a school for wealthy Maryland boys, the most notorious of whom was John Wilkes Booth. What did that young man learn here? We pondered that question while seated on comfy leather sofas in the cozy lounge. We were invited to sample a most unusual Wassail Punch being served to a private party in an adjoining dining room. Just one sip convinced us this was a "must" recipe to use for celebrations.

Soon our table in the Cardinal Dining Room was ready. The original wide-planked wood floors hummed beneath our footsteps as we were led to a table, covered with a wine-colored cloth, beside the room's fireplace. Keeping to the menu's light side, I chose the salad named after the inn's

118

proprietor, Eleanora. The salad's tangy dressing had the appropriate zip to enhance the varied greens without over-powering the hearts of palm. Since Rebecca has a hard time passing up fresh seafood, she chose the Shrimp Salad. My daughter Daintry rarely allows a Sirloin Steak Sandwich to pass her by, and this time was no exception.

In between bites we learned that the boys' school had been named Milton after the poet John Milton, author of *Paradise Lost*. The curriculum included Greek, Latin and English classics—hardly the fodder for budding assassins, so Booth was no doubt influenced elsewhere.

Before leaving, we were given a tour of their famed wine cellar, where guests are invited to peruse the enormous connossieur selection. Although we weren't going to have an after-dinner drink, it was difficult to bypass a choice concoc-tion by the late owner, Atillio Allori. Hence, we were into-duced to "Leo's" Kiss, and we must admit it was an ideal way to say goodbye.

Milton Inn is located at 14833 on York Road in Sparks. Lunch is served from noon until 2:30 p.m., Monday through Friday. Dinner is from 6:00 p.m. until 10:00 p.m., Monday through Friday, and from 6:00 p.m. until 11:00 p.m. on Sat-urday. For reservations (recommended) call (301) 771-4366.

MILTON INN'S WASSAIL PUNCH

1 cup superfine sugar	48 whole cloves
6 to 7 cinnamon sticks	juice of 1 large orange
1 lemon, sliced	juice of 1 lime
1/2 cup water	1 gallon good Burgundy
1 gallon apple cider	wine
1 gallon cranberry juice	

In a small saucepan boil the sugar, cinnamon sticks, and lemon slices in water for 3 to 4 minutes; strain, discarding lemon slices. Into a large pot pour the apple cider, cranberry juice, cloves, orange juice, lime juice and strained cinnamon mixture and simmer for 30 minutes. Garnish punch with

119

orange slices. Before serving add Burgundy and stir. Ladle into punch cups. Yields 3 gallons (96-half cup servings).

MILTON INN'S LEO'S KISS

½ ounce Amaretto
½ ounce white Creme de
Cacao

½ ounce white Creme de
Menthe

Pour all ingredients into a small brandy snifter or a 2-ounce glass and stir to combine flavors. Serves 1.

MILTON INN'S "ELEANORA" SALAD

1 bunch watercress
1 14-ounce can hearts of
palm
½ head of Belgian endive
lettuce

¼ pound fresh mushrooms,
sliced
salt and pepper to taste

Wash watercress and trim away all but leafy portion; place in a salad bowl. Add drained hearts of palm, washed Belgian endive and mushrooms. Toss to combine and add salt and pepper. Add dressing (recipe below) and serve. Serves 4 to 6.

Dressing:
1 tablespoon dried tarragon
⅓ cup red wine vinegar
¾ cup vegetable oil

1 teaspoon Dijon mustard
1 egg
juice of ½ lemon

Place all ingredients in blender or food processor and blend until well mixed. Yields over 1 cup.

THE MANOR TAVERN
Monkton

THE MANOR
TAVERN

I tell you, some women have all the luck. In 1667, Charles Calvert, the third Lord Baltimore, was riding through a lush area of Maryland on his way to smoke the peace pipe with the Indians when he made the sage decision to retain 10,000 acres of "this faire land." In 1713, he made a gift of the land to his fourth bride and specified that it be called "My Lady's Manor." That lady was indeed lucky to receive this parcel of land, which was once the rich hunting and camping ground of the Piscataway Indians, the southern branch of the powerful Susquehanna tribe. I'm sure she'd be pleased today with the quaint restaurant, The Manor Tavern, located on "her" property.

Rebecca, Daintry and I traveled on the Old York Road through this fairyland that was in the process of giving birth to spring. Originally an Indian trail, the Old York Road became the main north-south thoroughfare as traffic through the colonies progressed. Many shops, taverns and stables were built after nearby St. James Church was begun in 1750. The Manor Tavern was a stable during that period, serving both the customers of Slade's Tavern, located directly across the road, and the parishioners of the church.

The restaurant's cuisine is split between fancy French and regional Maryland, and the décor is a subtle blend of rustic and "citified" in this land of fast horses and clever foxes. In a restaurant that treads so many delicate center lines, the house rosé seemed the appropriate choice to accompany our appetizers of juicy Escargot Champignon and Clams Casino.

After a Caesar Salad, dramatically prepared tableside, we enjoyed a delicious entrée called My Lady's Choice. This savory dish is a classed-up country veal sautéed with Smithfield ham and crabmeat, then dressed in a creamy Mornay Sauce.

Although it was early for outside dining, Spring's visitation lured us to their patio for dessert. I ordered the steaming hot Bread Pudding smothered in a wondrous rich Lemon Rum Sauce while we watched the tableside preparation of Cherries Jubilee.

122

Fine food and gentrified revelry isn't the tavern's only claim to fame. Between 1773 and 1781, on his frequent trips between Mount Vernon and Philadelphia, George Washington patronized Slade's Tavern. The Manor Tavern doesn't claim that "Washington slept here," but they are proud to have had his horse as one of their first guests.

The Manor Tavern is located on Route 138 in Monkton. Lunch is served from 11:30 a.m. until 3:00 p.m., Monday through Saturday. Dinner is served from 5:30 p.m. until 10:00 p.m., Tuesday through Saturday, and from 4:00 p.m. until 9:00 p.m. on Sunday. Sunday brunch is served from noon until 3:00 p.m. For reservations (recommended) call (301) 771-4840.

THE MANOR TAVERN'S MY LADY'S CHOICE

4 4-ounce medallions of veal
2 eggs, beaten
¾ cup Italian-seasoned bread crumbs
3 tablespoons butter
1 cup white wine
4 3-ounce slices Smithfield ham
8 ounces lump crabmeat
Mornay Sauce (recipe below)

Pound veal with a meat mallet until thin. Dip veal in beaten eggs and coat with bread crumbs. In a large skillet melt butter and sauté veal over high heat. Drain excess butter and set veal aside in warm place. Deglaze skillet by adding wine. Reduce heat to simmer and add ham and crabmeat. Cook about 2 minutes. On 4 warmed plates place veal and top each portion with ham and equal portion of crabmeat. Lace the top with Mornay Sauce. Serves 4.

Mornay Sauce:
2 tablespoons butter
2 tablespoons all-purpose flour
1 cup milk
2 ounces Swiss cheese, grated
2 ounces Cheddar cheese, grated
2 ounces Parmesan cheese, grated

123

Melt butter in a saucepan; add flour and stir into a paste. Add milk, stirring until smooth. Add cheeses and stir until melted and incorporated into sauce. Yields about 1½ cups.

THE MANOR TAVERN'S BREAD PUDDING IN LEMON RUM SAUCE

1½ cups bread crumbs
2 cups buttermilk, scalded
2 eggs
1 cup brown sugar
1 cup all-purpose flour
1 teaspoon baking soda
1 teaspoon nutmeg

¼ teaspoon salt
1 cup raisins
1 cup pecans, broken in
  pieces
Lemon Rum Sauce (recipe
  below)

Soak bread crumbs in scalded buttermilk for 15 minutes. Meanwhile, beat eggs until creamy and add sugar gradually. Combine flour, baking soda, nutmeg and salt and stir into egg mixture. Combine with bread crumb mixture and stir in raisins and pecans. Spoon into a 2-quart greased baking dish. Place dish in a pan of hot water and bake in a 350-degree oven for 50 minutes or until inserted knife comes out clean. Top with Lemon Rum Sauce. Serves 8 to 10.

Lemon Rum Sauce:
½ cup raisins
2 cups water
½ cup sugar
½ cup dark rum

1 tablespoon cornstarch
juice of 2 lemons
grated rind of 1 lemon

Cook raisins in water until tender. Remove from heat and drain all but ½ cup water. To the same pan add sugar and rum. In a separate bowl, dissolve cornstarch in lemon juice. Add lemon juice mixture and rind of 1 lemon to pan. Simmer over low heat, stirring until blended. Serve over pudding.

COCKEY'S TAVERN
Westminster

COCKEY'S TAVERN

Would the South have won more battles if the illustrious J. E. B. Stuart and his Confederate troops had pursued the Union soldiers rather than the maids at Cockey's Tavern? The legend is that the troops enjoyed more than room and board when they stayed at the tavern during a skirmish with Union forces in the neighborhood in 1863.

Twenty-five years earlier, the tavern had been Dr. William Willis' handsome brick residence and the meeting place for the first session of circuit court in the newly formed Carroll County. Other guests in the history of Cockey's Tavern were travelers on the Baltimore-Pittsburgh Stagecoach and poker players whose stakes were sometimes whole herds of cattle that changed hands overnight.

Those gamblers, of course, wouldn't recognize the place today, although the lounge has original dentil work, raised paneling and one of the house's prized bay windows. Walls are covered with portraits of nineteenth-century families and famous people. These paintings take a mysterious tumble now and then, suggesting the presence of a ghost. It would be easy to pick a target, since diners usually claim the same seats each time they visit. General Grant's picture fell one day on a lawyer who regularly lunches in the room next to the lounge.

Having heard that story, Gordon and I sat at a table where we could keep an eye on General Grant in the dining room and General Stuart at the bar (a converted church pew). It seemed appropriate in a high-stakes place to order Clams Casino, which were cooked in butter with spring onions—an ingredient often specified in recipes at Cockey's Tavern.

The chef describes the restaurant's cuisine as American but says his background is classical French. Having apprenticed under a chef who served both General DeGaulle and Jacqueline Kennedy, he now teaches a gourmet cooking class. I picked up a wonderful lesson on making pie dough. I was eager to get home and try the technique—putting the flour and frozen margarine into a food processor and taking out a smooth dough, half of which (the upper crust) is then rolled in sugar. I'm delighted to say it worked. Fruit pies made this way at Cockey's are blueberry, peach and apple. I used peaches, cut in halves as the chef suggested.

Of the Veal Normande, the chef says, "Let the veal speak for itself." And who needs to say more about veal scalloppine with mushrooms, cream and white wine—provided there's a little spring onion.

Cockey's Tavern is located at 216 East Main Street in Westminster. Meals are served from 11:00 a.m. until 10:00 p.m., Monday through Friday; from 3:00 p.m. until 11:00 p.m. on Saturday; and from noon until 8:00 p.m. on Sunday. For reservations (recommended) call (301) 848-4202.

COCKEY'S TAVERN'S PEACH PIE

Crust:

3 cups all-purpose flour   flour and sugar for rolling
1 cup margarine, frozen   dough
⅓ cup very cold water

Put flour in food processor. Leave it "on" (highest speed available) and add small pieces of margarine, a little at a time. Allow 30 seconds for margarine to break up; then add water in a slow, steady stream. Dough will bind itself together and form a ball. Divide dough into two parts. Roll bottom crust on a floured surface and fit it into a 9-inch pie pan. Roll both sides of remaining dough on a surface sprinkled with sugar, and set aside to use as upper crust.

Filling:

8 fresh peaches   3 tablespoons cornstarch
⅔ cup sugar
1 teaspoon cinnamon (or
   more)

Skin peaches, cut in halves and remove pits. Combine sugar, cinnamon and cornstarch, and toss peach halves in this mixture to coat thoroughly. Place coated halves in pie shell along with remaining sugar-cinnamon mixture. Fit sugared upper crust over filling. Bake in a 350-degree oven for 1 hour or until sugar browns on top. (Do not overcook fruit.) Yields 1 covered 9-inch pie.

COCKEY'S TAVERN'S VEAL NORMANDE

4 tablespoons butter
1 pound veal scallopine
flour for dusting
12 mushrooms, sliced thin

4 spring onions, sliced thin
8 ounces white wine
8 ounces heavy cream

Melt butter in a heavy skillet, heating until very hot. Dust veal lightly with flour and sauté in hot butter for 1 minute on each side. Remove veal to a warm platter. Add mushrooms, spring onions and wine to pan, raise heat and boil about 1 minute. Add cream and boil again, stirring, for 1 minute or until sauce thickens. Pour sauce over veal and serve immediately. Serves 4.

COCKEY'S TAVERN'S CLAMS CASINO

Casino Butter:
½ pound soft butter
3 spring onions, chopped
½ medium green pepper,
  finely diced

4 ounces pimento, chopped
juice of ½ lemon
1 garlic clove

Combine all ingredients and mix well.

6 strips bacon

24 clams on half shells

Cut each bacon strip crosswise into 4 pieces. Place 1 rounded teaspoonful of Casino Butter over each clam, and cover with one piece of bacon. Bake in a very hot oven (450 to 475 degrees) for 5 to 7 minutes, or broil for 4 to 5 minutes, until bacon is crisp. Yields 4 to 6 appetizer servings.

MAGGIE'S
Westminster

MAGGIE'S

Rounding a bend in the road one night, Gordon and I discovered Maggie's. The date "1903" caught my eye, so we stopped to go into the barroom that was originally operated by Maggie and Levi Zahn. Before their time, the building had been a store for tools and farm implements, with the owner backpacking through the valleys around Westminster to reach his customers.

During the Zahns' lifetime, Maggie ran the bar and Levi ran a blacksmith's shop in the back of the building. For several decades, except during Prohibition, Maggie's continued to sell drinks. Later, as the Green Street Inn, it reportedly served the best steamed crabs ever eaten. After other owners and vacancies, the building was bought and reopened in 1976 as Maggie's. The name was restored because the owner had childhood recollections of Maggie, whom he remembered as the woman who always wore a black apron. When Maggie's remodeled the former blacksmith's shop into a dining room, the hearth and fireplace were styled to look like the type Levi might have used.

Maggie's prides itself on having casual charm and a menu that's both Continental and traditional Maryland. It was after the dinner hour, so I had to be content with an imaginary order for a luncheon dish listed on the menu as one of "Maggie's Favorites," Chicken Livers with Mushrooms and Tomatoes. The waitress said, "That's *everybody's* favorite." Gordon said his choice would have been Chicken Champagne—strips of chicken fillet and julienne carrots with sliced mushrooms in a champagne gravy. The recipe for Brussel Sprouts Dijonnaise gives us a new way to fix an old favorite vegetable by serving brussel sprouts in a sauce of mustard and cream.

A room with off-white walls, a brick floor, exposed wood and lots of plants is called the Ivan Gamber room because of a nameplate that hangs there. The wooden sign had been found in the attic, but no one knew who Ivan Gamber was until the ninety-year-old man walked in a few years ago. Probably curiosity brought him to the place where he had worked for Levi as a blacksmith (until automobiles became popular and he switched to repairing cars). Ivan liked Maggie's—and the sign with his name on it—so much that he stayed for lunch!

Maggie's is located on Washington Road (Route 32) at Green Street in Westminster. Brunch is served from 11:00 a.m. until 3:00 p.m. on Sunday. Lunch is served from 11:00 a.m. until 4:00 p.m., daily. Dinner is served from 5:00 p.m. until 10:00 p.m., daily. For reservations (recommended) call (301) 848-1441 or (301) 876-6868.

MAGGIE'S BRUSSEL SPROUTS DIJONNAISE

1 pint fresh brussel sprouts	1½ to 2 tablespoons Dijon
1½ tablespoons butter	mustard
¼ cup chicken stock	salt and pepper to taste
¾ cup whipping cream	bacon bits or parsley

Wash and trim brussel sprouts, cut an "x" in bottoms with paring knife, and blanch in lightly salted water until tender. Drain. In a skillet, melt butter over medium heat. Add brussel sprouts and cook until warmed through. Increase heat to high, add chicken stock and reduce by half. Stir in cream and mustard. Bring to a rapid boil and reduce until sauce coats a wooden spoon. Add salt and pepper to taste. Brussel sprouts may be topped with crisp bacon bits and fresh chopped parsley. Serves 4.

MAGGIE'S CHICKEN LIVERS WITH MUSHROOMS AND TOMATOES

oil to coat skillet	1 14-ounce can plum
½ cup flour for dredging	tomatoes
1½ pounds fresh chicken	2 garlic cloves, minced
livers	¼ cup dry sherry
6 shallots, diced (or use 1	2 cups brown sauce or Jus
small red onion)	Lie (see note)
½ pound fresh mushrooms,	salt and pepper to taste
sliced	cooked rice for 6

131

Heat oil in heavy skillet. Dredge chicken livers lightly in flour and sauté until brown and slightly crisp, approximately 5 minutes. Remove from skillet to a warm, covered platter. Drain oil from pan, and add shallots, mushrooms, tomatoes and garlic. Cook until mushrooms become tender. Turn heat to high, add sherry and ignite. Bring to a rapid boil, and add brown sauce or Jus Lie and livers. Simmer for approximately 5 minutes over medium heat. Add salt and pepper to taste, and serve over rice. Serves 4 to 6.

Note: To make 2 cups of Jus Lie, melt 4 tablespoons of butter in skillet, add 4 tablespoons of flour and stir until there is a smooth roux. Add 12 ounces of canned beef broth, a little at a time, stirring to keep sauce smooth.

MAGGIE'S CHICKEN CHAMPAGNE

1½ pounds boneless chicken breasts
⅓ cup flour for dredging
⅓ cup oil
4 tablespoons butter
4 medium carrots, peeled, julienned and blanched
½ pound mushrooms, sliced
8 shallots, sliced
1 cup champagne
½ cup dry sherry
1½ cups whipping cream
salt and pepper to taste
fresh parsley for garnish

Cut chicken (trimmed of any fat) into strips approximately 1½ by 3 inches and lightly dust with flour. Heat oil in skillet, then add chicken and sauté approximately 2 minutes on each side; remove to warm platter. Drain oil from skillet and add butter. Sauté carrots, mushrooms and shallots until tender. Turn heat to high, and add champagne and sherry. Boil until reduced by half. Add cream and stir to blend. Lower heat and cook until sauce lightly coats a wooden spoon. Add salt and pepper to taste. Pour sauce over chicken. Garnish with sprigs of fresh parsley. Serves 6.

Note: Look in gourmet stores for champagne in 8-ounce bottles, the right amount for this recipe.

MEALEY'S
New Market

MEALEY'S

New Market so prides itself on being the antique capital that no new commercial shops are allowed to open if offering anything other than antiques. Keeping in perfect step with this preservation of the past is Mealey's, circa 1800. Operating originally as an inn, the building has seen many occupants come and go.

In 1905, several upstairs bedrooms were converted into offices for the C and P Telephone Company. At that time, the inn was known as the Utz Hotel. An Utz granddaughter remembers the tale that her mother loved to tell about her own employment at the telephone company. It seems that at age nine, when not in school, she worked as a relief operator. It gave her status among other children, especially when she could brag to her friends about having to be hidden when the telephone company supervisors from the Baltimore office suddenly materialized for on-site inspections.

Nothing remains of the old telephone operation except a few telephones that are displayed in the downstairs dining rooms where Rebecca, Daintry and I had lunch. In our dining adventures we explore many varied cuisines, so it was great fun to happen onto the country-style fixin's at Mealey's.

Daintry and Becca liked their homemade Coleslaw, while I had a fit over their Green Beans, prepared with country ham and tasting exactly like my grandmother's. Although it may not sound like a country dish, their Old Fashioned Club Sandwich is definitely old-timey. It is a hot open-face club sandwich smothered in a cheese and mushroom sauce. They use regular rather than country ham in this preparation because, as manager Jim Jeffries says, "City folks just don't know how to appreciate the country ham." However, country ham is offered on their menu for those who appreciate the saltier flavor.

We chose iced tea after Jeffries told us about a mishap that occurred when former owner Dick Mealey invited Washington dignitaries to dine at the restaurant. Wanting the meal to be special, Mrs. Mealey served Dick's homemade wine.

Unfortunately, those were Prohibition days, and it so happened that an Internal Revenue employee was in the party. A few days later, wine disappeared from the premises.

Wine is available today, but Jeffries says, "It's not a big thing with us. We concentrate more earnestly on our home-style country cooking. To do this right, you've got to use old-fashioned lard in an iron skillet to fry your chicken." Mostly because of the preparation, Chicken Livers is one of their most requested dishes.

Wanting to experience more of the flavor of this restaurant, we moved into the Pump Room for our dessert of delicious homebaked Pecan Pie. The old water pump standing in the rear of the room was originally the hotel's only water supply. It boggles my mind to think of the time and energy involved in operating this device for a whole inn full of people.

In the adjoining barroom we saw an old Wurlitzer juke-box. Someone put a nickel in just as we were leaving, and we departed to the strains of *It Might As Well Be Spring*, which was thoroughly appropriate as it was a lovely Maryland spring day.

Mealey's is located at 8 Main Street in New Market. Lunch is served from 11:30 a.m. until 3:00 p.m., Tuesday through Saturday. Dinner is served from 5:00 p.m. until 9:00 p.m., Monday through Saturday. Sunday dinner is served from 11:30 a.m. until 8:00 p.m. For reservations call (301) 865-5488.

MEALEY'S PECAN PIE

4 eggs	4 tablespoons melted butter
1 cup sugar	2 teaspoons vanilla
1 cup dark corn syrup	1 cup pecans
1 tablespoon flour	1 unbaked 9-inch pie shell
1/2 teaspoon salt	

Beat eggs by hand. Add sugar and whip together with electric mixer. Add syrup and mix until combined. Add flour and salt, whipping until combined, and blend in melted butter. Add vanilla and mix until incorporated. Fold in

135

pecans and pour into pie shell. Bake in a 350-degree oven for 50 minutes or until knife inserted in center comes out clean. Yields 1 pie.

MEALEY'S OLD FASHIONED CLUB SANDWICH

Sauce:

2 tablespoons butter	1/2 cup grated Cheddar
2 tablespoons plain flour	cheese
1 cup milk	
1 10-ounce can mushroom soup	

In a skillet melt butter over medium high heat. Add flour and stir until a paste forms. Add milk and stir until mixture is combined. Add mushroom soup and stir until blended. Add cheese and stir until melted.

8 slices white bread	8 slices tomato
8 thin slices ham	8 slices fried bacon
8 thin slices turkey	

Lay the slices of bread in a large, flat pan and cover each slice with equal portions of ham, turkey and tomato. Ladle sauce over all and heat in a 375-degree oven for 5 minutes. Serve 2 open-faced sandwiches on each plate, topped with bacon. Serves 4.

MEALEY'S COLESLAW

1 small cabbage	1 tablespoon cider vinegar
1/2 cup mayonnaise	1/2 teaspoon salt
1 tablespoon sugar	1/2 teaspoon pepper
1/4 cup evaporated milk	

Shred cabbage. Add remaining ingredients and correct seasoning to taste. Cover and refrigerate. Serves 4 to 6.

BUSHWALLER'S
Frederick

BUSHWALLER'S

Frederick is a town that honors her historical past without losing place with the pace of her future. You are firmly anchored in both periods when you dine at Bushwaller's. Familiar dishes are served in innovative ways, such as the sandwiches that are garnished with fresh vegetables rather than the traditional chips or fries. For history's sake, however, each sandwich is named for a famous Frederick character or event. The R.B. Taney, a rich and juicy combination of beef and cheese slipped between artichokes, was my sampling choice, while Jubal Early Bird won the story choice.

The latter sandwich is named after the confederate general Jubal Early, who threatened to burn Frederick unless his ransom was met. So, the city fathers gathered bushel baskets of money and left them on the steps of the city hall. As a transplanted Westerner who grew up in the South, I find it funny that Southern history books depicted only the Yankees using those tactics. Hmmm.

One of the charms of Frederick is that it has kept its early Federal-style village atmosphere. Bushwaller's, which now recaptures the feeling of a neighborhood tavern, was built as a private home in 1840. Sometime around the turn of the century, the home became Steiner's Drug Store. It later became a dry goods store dealing in contraband cigarettes, and when the Bushwaller brothers found it in 1980, it had become a liquor store.

Like the sandwich dishes, their Sautéed Chicken Breast was as attractive to look at as it was to taste. My chicken, which was light and luscious, was complemented by wild rice and fresh steamed asparagus plus accents of fresh strawberries.

Dieters may be lucky enough to order Alligator Tail, which tastes like veal, is very short on calories, and is served when obtainable. Or you can always lunch on Hearts of Palm Salad or Seafood Marinade to keep your jeans from pinching. However, it won't help if, like me, you take in their wonderful Strawberry or famous Mud Pie for dessert.

138

Anyone who finds himself near Frederick on St. Patrick's Day should join in what they call the "Pub Crawl." All true or adopted Irish gather together, not to charm the snakes, as St. Paddy did on the celebrated day, but to travel together in the most outlandish costumes that can be assembled. Walking from restaurant to restaurant demands lots of energy, and the throng insists that certain libations are necessary for the pilgrimage.

Bushwaller's is located at 209 North Market Street in Frederick. Lunch is served from 11:30 a.m. until 4:00 p.m., and dinner from 5:00 p.m. until 10:00 p.m., daily. For reservations (recommended) call (301) 694-5697.

BUSHWALLER'S R.B. TANEY'S SANDWICH

1 tablespoon horseradish
1 tablespoon sour cream
salt and pepper to taste
1 hard roll
2 to 3 slices rare roast beef, cooked

2 artichoke hearts, sliced in half
2 slices Swiss cheese

Mix horseradish with sour cream, salt and pepper. Slice hard roll in half and spread both sides with horseradish mixture. Layer roast beef, artichoke hearts and Swiss cheese on bottom half of roll, cover with top half and heat in a 400-degree oven for 5 minutes. Serves 1.

BUSHWALLER'S SAUTEED CHICKEN BREAST

4 boneless chicken breasts
flour for dredging
salt and pepper to taste
3 tablespoons butter
12 fresh mushrooms, sliced
4 pimentos, sliced fine
4 sprigs parsley, chopped fine

heavy pinch of garlic powder
dash of salt
dash of pepper
1/4 cup white wine
1 tablespoon sour cream
wild rice, cooked according to package directions

Pound chicken breasts lightly with a meat mallet and dredge in flour seasoned with salt and pepper. Melt butter in skillet over high heat and sauté chicken on both sides until cooked. Remove chicken and keep warm. Add mushrooms, pimentos, parsley, garlic, salt and pepper and sauté until tender, adding more butter if needed. Stir in wine and cook for 4 to 5 minutes. Add sour cream and stir until well blended. Serve chicken with wild rice. Ladle sauce over chicken. Serves 4.

BUSHWALLER'S BEEF AND SCALLOPS SAUTE

1 pound beef tenderloin
flour for dredging
salt and pepper to taste
2 tablespoons virgin olive
  oil
1 to 2 tablespoons butter
3/4 pound sea scallops
24 fresh mushrooms, sliced
1 cup red wine

2 teaspoons lemon juice
1 teaspoon dried basil or 10
  fresh basil leaves,
  chopped
1/2 cup beef consommé
1 garlic clove, crushed
parsley and chopped
  scallions for garnish

Trim beef and slice thin. Dredge in flour seasoned with salt and pepper. Melt olive oil and butter in skillet over high heat and sauté beef on both sides. Add scallops and mushrooms and sauté about 2 minutes or until scallops are done. Remove beef, scallops and mushrooms and keep warm. Deglaze pan by adding wine. After boiling for 1 to 2 minutes, reduce heat and add lemon juice, basil, consommé and garlic. Stir and cook for 7 to 9 minutes to allow flavors to develop. Place beef, scallops and mushrooms on plates and ladle sauce on top. Garnish with parsley and scallions. Serves 4.

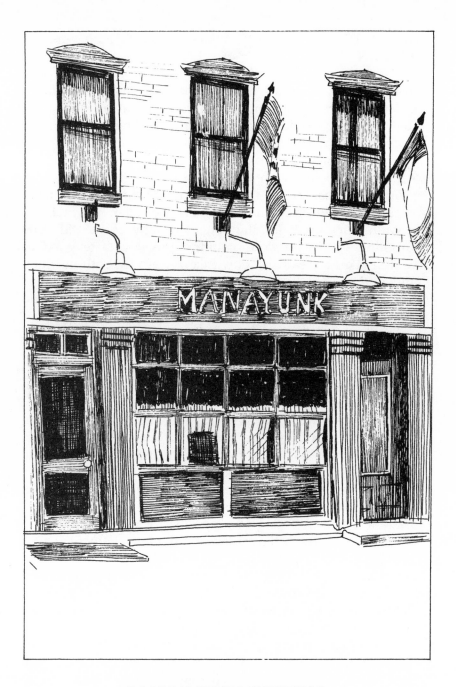

MANAYUNK TAVERN
Frederick

MANAYUNK TAVERN

Since the word "manayunk" is a Lenape Indian word meaning "the place to come and drink," anyone would naturally assume that a restaurant called Manayunk Tavern specializes in liquid offerings. Actually, Rebecca Schenck and I found nothing to be further from the truth. The tavern does have a bar and they do serve spirits, but for us, Manayunk was a celebration of the New American Cuisine, with a delicious accent on vegetables.

For some reason, too many restaurants short-change fresh vegetables, adding them only for color or filler. Maybe those restaurateurs grew up thinking, as many of us did, that anything "good for you" couldn't possibly taste good as well. It takes a creative chef with a concern for both nutrition and flavor to awaken one's taste buds to the possibilities of fresh vegetables. Such an awakening will occur when you dine at Manayunk Tavern.

This building has seen many commercial ventures since it was built in the 1880s. It seems to have come full circle, starting out as grocery store, then a machine shop and later a furniture store. Today the emphasis is once again on food in this historic building that is now a restaurant.

The furnishings are recycled architecture. For instance, the dark green booth where we dined was once an ornate window frame. When we asked why they had chosen to decorate with these pieces, manager Don Leedy replied, "If a piece is eighty to ninety years old and in good shape, it probably has the integrity to stick around for a while longer."

Rather than adhering to a specific theme, the décor encompasses anything that appeals to the management as well as the clientele. The fact that Leedy spent a lot of time in Iran is reflected in the décor. His Middle Eastern experiences also influence certain dishes, particularly the Lamb Bandit Style. Plucked from that area of the world and then modified for American tastes, the dish maintains a distinctive savor.

In the main dining room, an assemblage of international flags hang from the hand-hewn ceiling beams. Most of them have been contributed by customers. When you chomp down on Asparagus in Fillo or Brussels Sprouts in Fennel, you'll agree that this food is worth waving a flag over.

Manayunk does something very special for anyone with dietary restrictions. The chef is called to the customer's table, the problem is discussed, and the meal is prepared without guesswork. This careful approach is possible because the restaurant grows its own herbs, and their fish, fowl and beef are always the freshest.

It's true, dieters might have to sidestep their marvelous Almond Amaretto Cheesecake, but you could satisfy your sweet tooth with seasonal fresh fruit sans sauce.

Manayunk Tavern is located at 207 West Patrick Street in Frederick. Lunch is served from 11:30 a.m. until 2:30 p.m., daily. Dinner is from 5:00 p.m. until 10:00 p.m., Monday through Thursday; from 6:00 p.m. until 11:00 p.m., Friday and Saturday; and from 4:00 p.m. until 10:00 p.m. on Sunday. For reservations call (301) 662-0373.

MANAYUNK TAVERN'S LAMB BANDIT STYLE

1½ pounds shoulder lamb chops
2 to 3 tablespoons oil
2 tablespoons butter
2 medium onions, chopped
¾ teaspoon oregano
¾ teaspoon black pepper
2 sheets fillo pastry
½ cup melted butter
8 slices ripe tomato
4 slices Feta cheese, ¼ inch thick

Remove bone and any outside fat from lamb chops. Put oil in skillet and braise the lamb until brown. Remove and drain chops on paper towels. Melt butter in skillet and sauté onions until they are clear. Add oregano and pepper; stir and set aside. Cut fillo into 4 equal sections and brush each section with butter. Divide lamb equally and place each portion in center of a fillo sheet. Top each with 2 slices of tomato, a slice of Feta cheese and an equal portion of onions. Fold in sides of fillo; fold one end over the other and brush with butter. Place in a greased baking dish. Bake in a 350-degree oven for 8 minutes. Serves 4.

143

MANAYUNK TAVERN'S BRUSSEL SPROUTS
IN FENNEL

10 ounces fresh brussel
  sprouts
2 tablespoons olive oil

1 teaspoon fennel seed
2 tablespoons butter
salt and pepper

Cut stems from brussel sprouts, cutting an "x" in the bottom of each sprout. Steam for 10 minutes or until barely tender. Remove and cool to room temperature. In a small skillet heat the oil and add the fennel seed, stirring until lightly browned. Drain off the olive oil, saving fennel in skillet. Add butter to skillet, turn off heat, and stir until butter is melted. Add salt and pepper to taste. Pour butter-fennel mixture over brussel sprouts. Serves 4.

MANAYUNK TAVERN'S ASPARAGUS IN FILLO

8 fresh steamed asparagus
  spears
2 sheets fillo pastry
½ cup melted butter
4 tablespoons grated
  Romano cheese

4 tablespoons grated
  Gruyère cheese
4 tablespoons sliced
  almonds
Hollandaise sauce (mix or
  homemade)

Cut white ends from asparagus and steam until bright green. Cut sheets of fillo in half horizontally. Brush top two-thirds of each sheet with butter. On lower third of each sheet, sprinkle 1 tablespoon Romano cheese, 1 tablespoon Gruyère cheese and 1 tablespoon sliced almonds. Place 2 asparagus spears on top of cheese mixture; fold in sides of fillo and roll up. Brush outside of fillo with butter and place on a small, buttered, stainless steel or aluminum baking sheet. Repeat process with remaining ingredients to make three more rolls. Bake in a 350-degree oven for about 5 minutes or until brown. Top with Hollandaise sauce. Serves 4.

THE PROVINCE
Frederick

THE PROVINCE

No hats were on sale when I ate lunch in the former Mrs. Snyder's Hat Shop, but several women from Frederick told me they remembered when their mothers shopped here for their Sunday best. Those were the days of Mr. John's Originals, and local milliners fashioned ribbons and lace into imaginative designs. Then, alas, hats went out of style.

The property on North Market was first deeded to blacksmith Cudlip Miller, who passed it on to his son with the stipulation that rooms be added to the one-room home. The hat shop occupied the building some years back, but today a restaurant incorporates the original house and its additions. The restaurant is called The Province, Circa 1767. The word "province" refers to Maryland's having been a province, rather than a state, before the Revolutionary War.

On my tour of The Province, I was taken through the former hat shop into the original room, whose brick walls were partly covered with quilts that served as both baffle and decoration. One prized quilt contained the names of all those employed at The Province at the time the quilt was sewn by the mother of the chef. Beyond that room was a garden room with snowshoe chairs on a brick floor, and on the patio, tea was brewing in the sun beside an herb garden.

After the tour, I was seated in the front room with a glass of Chablis to wait for lunch. Between times of welcoming her guests by name, manager Nancy Floria explained that she and her husband had wanted to have a really good place to eat without going into Washington. The Province was established when Frederick lacked such places. Now the surge of growth in the town would make Cudlip Miller proud.

The Province is best known for its desserts (whole cakes are available with notice to the chef). I was intrigued to hear about a wedding cake they made from seven different kinds of cheesecake. A prettier dessert tray I've never seen: Queen Mother Chocolate Almond Cake, Kahlúa Pecan Pie, Cheesecake with Lemon Glaze. I ate the recommended Mocha Nut Torte and was pleased with the creamy, crumbly choice. It

146

was a perfect finish to my meal of Parisian Poulet, a combination of chicken, mushrooms and Brie that is the most popular entrée at The Province. I served it and the torte when Dawn O'Brien and two other collaborators for this cookbook series came to my house for lunch. We ate and ate, then happily smiled for publicity pictures.

The Province is located at 129 North Market Street in Frederick. Lunch is served from 11:30 a.m. until 3:00 p.m., Tuesday through Friday. Brunch is served from 11:30 a.m. until 3:00 p.m. on Saturday and from 11:00 a.m. until 2:30 p.m. on Sunday. Dinner is served from 5:30 p.m. until 9:00 p.m., Tuesday through Thursday, and from 5:30 p.m. until 10:00 p.m. on Friday and Saturday. For reservations (requested) call (301) 663-1441.

THE PROVINCE'S MOCHA NUT TORTE

Torte:

6 eggs, separated
1 cup sugar
1/2 cup vanilla wafers, ground

1/4 cup flour
1 cup finely ground walnuts

Beat egg yolks until light; then add 3/4 cup sugar, mixing until thick and pale. Beat egg whites, gradually adding 1/4 cup sugar, until stiff. Sift together vanilla wafers and flour and add walnuts. Then add the nut-wafer mixture alternately with the egg white mixture into the egg yolk mixture. Turn into two 9-inch cake pans lined with unbuttered parchment paper. Bake in a 350-degree oven for 20 minutes or until cake tester comes out clean. Remove from pans and cool on rack.

Icing:

1/2 cup sugar
2 tablespoons cornstarch
1 cup strong coffee (cold)
1 ounce semisweet
    chocolate, melted

1 tablespoon butter
1 teaspoon vanilla
1 cup heavy cream
chocolate shavings for
    garnish

Mix sugar and cornstarch in saucepan. Gradually add the coffee and melted chocolate to sugar mixture. Bring to a boil and cook for one minute. Add butter and vanilla, then set aside to cool. When cake is ready to frost, whip cream until thick and fold into cooled mocha mix. Spread frosting on one layer, place other layer on top and spread remaining frosting. Sprinkle chocolate shavings over top. Refrigerate at least one hour before serving. Serves 10 to 12.

THE PROVINCE'S PARISIAN POULET

4 ounces clarified butter
2 whole chicken breasts
flour for dredging
1 egg, well beaten
1 cup sliced fresh
  mushrooms

salt and pepper
4 ounces ripened Brie
2 to 3 ounces Amontillado
  sherry
cooked rice or couscous

In a large skillet heat clarified butter until butter is hot but not smoking. Dip chicken in flour, then in beaten egg. Place each piece in skillet, one at a time, shaking skillet vigorously to prevent sticking. Brown on both sides. Remove chicken and set aside. Add mushrooms to skillet, lightly salt and pepper to taste, and sauté about 1 minute. Replace chicken in skillet and top each piece with a slice of Brie. Add sherry and ignite. Remove pan from heat. Cover pan for a moment to melt the cheese. Place enough chicken for each serving on a bed of rice or couscous, and pour mushroom mixture over chicken. Serves 2 (or more).

COZY RESTAURANT
Thurmont

COZY RESTAURANT Everyone has a different idea of "Shangri-La," and even one person's dream will vary depending on his needs. But the evening that I crossed the tiny bridge opposite the Cozy Restaurant and Motel's waterwheel and stepped into a bedroom suite where a crackling fire cut the evening's chill, I responded to the wind-down message. The rustic atmosphere of this establishment, nestled in the lap of the Catoctin Mountains, was what I needed.

Apparently it was also what was needed by the Russian entourage that accompanied Brezhnev to Camp David in 1979. The Cozy Restaurant and Motel is located just eight miles from Camp David, and Russian security came to check out the establishment. Owners Mary Freeze and her son Jerry tried to persuade the Russians to seek more luxurious accommodations, but it was too late—they had already tasted the Cozy's juicy steaks and northern Maryland country cooking. A direct telephone line to Moscow was installed. For over ten days the Russians made heavy use of the Carousel Dining Room's "Groaning Board," which is laden with sixty-five items, not counting the assortment of up to fifty-five homemade desserts.

As did the Russians, Rebecca, Daintry and I sat down to what Becca described as "one juicy steak." This came after nibbles of their Hot Apple Fritters and homebaked Pumpkin, Cinnamon and Raisin breads. We knew, after one taste, why their Corn Soup is legendary.

Although the Cozy's wine cellar contains many popular imported and domestic vintages, we chose a wine from their local Berrywine Vineyard. A semi-dry Berrywine Allegre was a pleasant, light accompaniment to their Delicious Roast Turkey. We also checked out their crisp Country Fried Chicken and the mildly cured Ham, which is neither too sweet nor too salty.

Each year, the Cozy sponsors a local bake-off, which features four new desserts for the public to judge each week. Luckily, we arrived on week seven of the eight-week contest.

From an array that included such award-winners as Chocolate Eclair Pie, Mexican Wedding Cake, Strawberry-Banana Cream Dessert, and Blueberry Cassis Pie, we sampled everything we could hold.

We took a tour and were surprised by the Cozy's great size. Mary Freeze, in her fifty plus years at the Cozy, has seen it grow from twelve stools to a seating of over six hundred. On the hall bulletin board, the collection of photos of film, press, sport and political celebrities who have discovered the Cozy continually grows.

The Cozy Restaurant is located at 105 Frederick Road in Thurmont. The following hours apply April through October but may vary at other times. Saturday and Sunday breakfast buffet is served from 8:00 a.m. until 11:00 a.m., and dinner from 11:30 a.m. until 9:00 p.m. Meals are served from 11:15 a.m. until 9:00 p.m., Monday through Thursday, and from 11:30 a.m. until 9:30 p.m., Friday and Saturday. To check on winter hours or to make reservations call (301) 271-7373.

COZY RESTAURANT'S CORN SOUP

7 cups turkey broth
  (commercial or
  homemade)
1 cup chopped celery
1 pound can whole-kernel
  corn
2 tablespoons butter
1/4 teaspoon pepper
1 tablespoon plus 2
  teaspoons sugar
1/4 teaspoon thyme

1/2 tablespoon parsley
1/2 tablespoon chicken
  bouillon
1/2 tablespoon Accent or
  monosodium glutamate
  (optional)
1 to 2 drops yellow food
  coloring (optional)
6 tablespoons flour
1 egg yolk

To a large soup pot add turkey broth with all ingredients except flour and egg yolk. Cook for 45 minutes, stirring often. Mix the flour with egg yolk and crumble on top of soup. Stir, and cook for 10 minutes more. Serves 6.

151

COZY RESTAURANT'S BLUEBERRY CASSIS PIE

Meringue Crust:

¼ teaspoon salt
1 teaspoon vanilla
4 large egg whites
1 cup sugar
1 teaspoon baking powder

1 cup graham cracker
crumbs
½ cup coconut
½ cup chopped filberts,
hazelnuts or walnuts

Add salt and vanilla to egg whites and beat until foamy. Add sugar in a slow stream and continue beating until shiny peaks form. Combine baking powder, crumbs, coconut and nuts and fold mixture into beaten egg whites. Spread gently in a well-greased and floured 9-inch pie tin. Make rim slightly higher than center. Bake at 350 degrees for 30 minutes and cool. Meringue crust will fill pie pan full. Add filling on top of crust.

Filling:

3 cups fresh or frozen
blueberries, unsweetened
1 cup sugar
3 tablespoons flour, or 4 for
fresh berries

¼ teaspoon salt
1 tablespoon lemon juice
2 tablespoons Creme de
Cassis
3 beaten egg yolks

Put berries, sugar, flour, salt, lemon juice, Creme de Cassis and egg yolks in top of double boiler over simmering water and cook, stirring gently, until thick. Spoon mixture onto crust, spreading evenly. Chill.

Topping:

1 cup heavy cream
1 to 3 tablespoons
confectioners' sugar

1 tablespoon Creme de
Cassis
candied violets or nuts

Whip cream and fold in sugar to taste; add Creme de Cassis. Spread mixture in mounds over filling. Garnish with candied violets or nuts. Yields 1 pie.

THE OTT HOUSE PUB AND RESTAURANT
Emmitsburg

THE OTT HOUSE PUB AND RESTAURANT

Was there a drugstore in your childhood with a catty-cornered entrance that made it more enticing? The front door of The Ott House Pub and Restaurant is on a forty-five-degree angle to Main Street. I don't know whether it's confusing to exit at 2:00 on Saturday morning and be less than perpendicular, but it's fun to enter on a slant at noon or 5:00 p.m.

The building on Center Square has also served as an ice cream parlor, a college snack bar and a grocery store since it was I. S. Annan & Brother Drygoods in 1906. Back when it was a day's ride from Baltimore to Emmitsburg and another day's ride to Hagerstown, the stagecoach stopped at Center Square. The location of Emmitsburg, just eight miles from Gettysburg, meant that soldiers from both North and South passed through the town at some time.

The Ott family established the pub and restaurant in 1970. Mr. Ott is interested in the construction of the nineteenth-century building. Original brickwork had been plastered over, and he measures some of the restoration by water marks around the building's foundation. Floor joists cut "long" are significant because the round saw wasn't invented until the 1840s.

The National Emergency Training Center for Firemen in Emmitsburg has become allied with The Ott House. In 1980, when its second class graduated, a fireman from Boulder, Colorado, gave a shoulder patch to The Ott House to remember him by. That started a collection that now has 900 patches from the uniforms of firemen from as far away as Australia, Guam and Greenland.

Firemen come for intensive two-week courses in such subjects as management and arson detection. They have little time for recreation, but The Ott House picks them up by bus and gives them regional food. They like Seafood Platters with French Fries and Applesauce. Another favorite is Sugar-Cured Ham. The Ott House rebakes hams in gingerale for several hours in a slow oven.

When I heard that Chili was a popular menu choice, I

154

thought surely theirs would be the two-alarm kind; but, of course, The Ott House wouldn't make those firemen work overtime. The Chili was plenty hot for me, though, and I asked for the recipe.

The Ott House also caters to skiers, who gather around its fireplace from December through February. Sometimes it has to put up customers who are stranded in a snowstorm.

Gordon and I ordered two of the hot drinks—Peppermint Cocoa and Hot Raspberry Delight—and pretended we'd been skiing. The pretty drinks are easy to make, and I recommend the taste of both, but the smell is even better. The drinks put us in the mood for Oysters Roberto, the baked oyster specialty that's named for Bob Ott.

Hanging behind the bar with the firemen's patches is a Certificate of Appreciation for The Ott House's treatment of those who are "tired, cold, hungry and sorely in need of pleasant company and conversation." That commendation agrees with the quote The Ott House uses from Samuel Johnson: "Nothing yet contrived by man produces as much happiness as a good tavern."

The Ott House Pub and Restaurant is located at 5 West Main Street in Emmitsburg. Hours are from 10:00 a.m. until 2:00 a.m., Monday through Saturday, and from noon until 2:00 a.m. on Sunday. Reservations are not necessary, but the phone number is (301) 447-2625.

THE OTT HOUSE PUB AND RESTAURANT'S
OYSTERS ROBERTO

4 oysters on half shell
4 teaspoons cocktail sauce
2 teaspoons Parmesan
  cheese
garlic salt

1 slice bacon, fried and
  quartered
4 teaspoons Mozzarella
  cheese

Place oysters on shells in baking dish. On each oyster put 1 teaspoon cocktail sauce, 1/2 teaspoon Parmesan, a dash of garlic salt, a quarter-slice of bacon and 1 teaspoon Mozzarella

155

cheese. Bake in a 500-degree oven for 3 to 5 minutes or until cheese melts. Yields 4 appetizers or 1 entrée serving.

THE OTT HOUSE PUB AND RESTAURANT'S CHILI

1 pound ground beef
1/2 small onion, chopped
1/4 cup diced hot cherry peppers
2 tablespoons juice from peppers
1 tablespoon chili powder
4 cups canned dark red kidney beans

2 cups canned crushed tomatoes
2 cups canned whole tomatoes, diced
few drops Tabasco sauce
salt and pepper to taste

Brown meat slowly in a heavy soup pot or Dutch oven. Add onion. Drain off any grease. Add remaining ingredients and simmer for about 2 hours, stirring occasionally. Serves 6.

THE OTT HOUSE PUB AND RESTAURANT'S HOT RASPBERRY DELIGHT

1 1/2 ounces raspberry liqueur
1 cup strong hot tea

dollop of whipped cream
dash of cinnamon

Add liqueur to cup of tea. Top with whipped cream and sprinkle with cinnamon. Serves 1.

THE OTT HOUSE PUB AND RESTAURANT'S PEPPERMINT COCOA

1 envelope instant hot chocolate

1 1/2 ounces Peppermint Schnapps
dollop of whipped cream

Prepare hot chocolate according to package directions. Add Peppermint Schnapps and top with whipped cream. Serves 1.

OLD SOUTH MOUNTAIN INN
Boonsboro

OLD SOUTH MOUNTAIN INN

As Daintry, Rebecca and I followed the ribbon of mountain road, we played the game of pretending we were travelers on this National Trail in the days of stagecoaches and wagons. The landscape surrounding the Old South Mountain Inn is dotted with few buildings even today, so it was easy to imagine how the sight of the inn must have quickened the heartbeats of eighteenth-century travelers in need of refuge. The 1732 Federalist-style stone structure, now painted white with bright red shutters and windowboxes full of geraniums, was a cheerful and welcome sight for us as well.

We decided the early spring sun was warm enough for an *al fresco* sampling of the local Byrd Vineyard's Chardonnay before lunch. Actually, I think we were a little overeager for the seasonal change, because once inside we were glad to be warmed by their thick, fresh, homemade Tomato Soup. Then, while Becca enjoyed their Soft-Shelled Maryland Crabs and Daintry tackled the German Wurst Plate, I couldn't stop munching on a Green Salad that was accompanied by the tangiest Curry Dressing.

We took our dessert in the lounge, which has been decorated to look much as you might imagine it looked over two hundred years ago. The recipe for rich, freshly made Apple Dapple Cake was, I learned, an adaptation of one that was used almost that long ago.

During the Civil War, this old building played a part in two notorious events. In 1859 the inn was captured and held overnight as an outpost and gathering place for John Brown's followers in the infamous raid on Harper's Ferry. Three years later, it was the headquarters of Confederate General D.H. Hill during the Battle of South Mountain, which was a preliminary to the Battle of Antietam.

Of course, an establishment like this has its ghost. In 1876 Mrs. Madeline Dahlgren purchased the inn and turned it into a private residence. It can't be proved, but the presence that wanders like a wisp of cold air through the upstairs is believed to be her spirit. Until recently the restaurant's chefs were given an upstairs room for convenience. According to the story, each was awakened so frequently by a knock at the door that produced nothing more than a cool breeze fleeing past, that they all decided that nearness to one's occupation isn't everything.

The Old South Mountain Inn is located on Alternate Route 40 between Boonsboro and Middletown. Dinner is served from 5:00 p.m. until 9:00 p.m., Tuesday through Friday. Saturday dining is from 11:30 a.m. until 10:00 p.m. Sunday brunch is served from 10:30 a.m. until 2:00 p.m., and Sunday dinner from noon until 8:00 p.m. For reservations (requested) call (301) 432-6155.

OLD SOUTH MOUNTAIN INN'S
APPLE DAPPLE CAKE

1½ cups vegetable oil
2 cups sugar
3 eggs
2 teaspoons vanilla
3 cups all-purpose flour
1 teaspoon salt
1 teaspoon baking soda

1½ cups chopped pecans
  (or less)
3 cups Stayman apples,
  peeled and chopped fine
sauce for topping (recipe
  below)

Cream oil, sugar, eggs and vanilla together with electric mixer. Sift together the flour, salt and baking soda. Add sifted ingredients gradually to egg mixture. Fold in nuts and apples. Bake in a greased tube pan for 1 hour at 350 degrees. When cake is done, do not remove from pan; pierce cake with a fork and spoon sauce over it while still hot. Keep cake in pan for 2 hours before serving. Yields 1 large cake.

Sauce:

1 cup light brown sugar
½ cup milk

1 stick butter or margarine

Place all ingredients in a saucepan and stir to combine. Continue cooking, stirring, over medium heat for 3 minutes.

159

OLD SOUTH MOUNTAIN INN'S
SOFT-SHELLED CRABS

2 tablespoons clarified
  butter
2 tablespoons oil (or more
  as needed)
1 large garlic clove, minced
3 medium shallots, chopped
  fine
3 tablespoons flour

1 teaspoon salt
1 teaspoon pepper
4 to 6 small soft-shelled
  crabs
½ cup white wine
  (Riesling)
½ cup sliced almonds
3 lemon wedges

Heat butter with oil in a large, heavy skillet over low heat. Sauté garlic and shallots, stirring constantly, until transparent. Combine flour, salt and pepper in a brown paper bag and toss crabs in the bag until coated. Place crabs upside down in a skillet and sauté over low heat until lightly browned on one side. Add ¼ cup of wine and continue to sauté for 3 minutes. Turn crabs over and add remaining wine. Sprinkle almonds over crabs, cover and simmer for 8 minutes. Serve with lemon wedges. Serves 3.

OLD SOUTH MOUNTAIN INN'S TOMATO SOUP

1 stick butter
3 chicken bouillon cubes
3 stalks celery, chopped
  fine
1 small onion, chopped fine
¼ cup flour

4 1-pound cans of tomatoes,
  chopped
3 to 4 cups tomato juice
1 5⅓-ounce can evaporated
  milk
salt and pepper to taste

Melt butter in a skillet with chicken bouillon, stirring to combine. Add celery and onions and sauté until tender. Stir in the flour to make a roux. Lower heat and cook for 10 minutes. Add chopped tomatoes plus juice from their cans along with tomato juice. Stir until well mixed, then stir in evaporated milk. Season with salt and pepper. Serves 10 to 12.

DUTCH KITCHEN
Hagerstown

DUTCH KITCHEN

When you're a stranger in town, wouldn't you give a pretty penny to know where the residents go for a good meal? In Hagerstown it's the Dutch Kitchen. Barry Tuckwell, Director of the Maryland Symphony, drops in when he's in town, and his photograph is among those that decorate one dining room. Betty Stahl, who owns and manages Dutch Kitchen with her husband Richard, regrets not getting a picture when Guy Lombardo came. She has one of Ernest Borgnine, but she doesn't need it to remember his kiss on her fiftieth birthday.

Dutch Kitchen calls itself "one of Maryland's oldest restaurants." Betty Stahl's grandmother remembered when a German delicatessen was in the building in the 1880s, and that predecessor probably inspired the name Dutch Kitchen.

The building resembles a Bavarian cottage, and plaques on the walls pay homage to Friendship, Liberty and Musick. Hagerstown "enjoys a long time friendship with the past," said an article in the twenty-five-year-old *Woman's Day* magazine Betty showed me. The article commended Dutch Kitchen on its oysters, for which they are still famous.

It was the beginning of the oyster season when I was there, and I would have loved a Fried Count Oyster sandwich for lunch, but the Stahls weren't satisfied with the big oysters yet and didn't want to dissatisfy customers who look forward to eating them at Dutch Kitchen. "Count" means 100 oysters to a gallon and two to a sandwich. Although I had to wait for a taste, I learned how the restaurant prepares count oysters. When Betty mentioned coating the oysters and laying them on a tray in the refrigerator, I thought about the story of a father who instructed his daughters to place oysters "shoulder to shoulder" between layers of bread crumbs. The girls always wondered how to tell which part of the oyster was the shoulder.

Regular customers hope for a Country Ham Sandwich every other week. When enough ham accumulates from hocks boiled for the popular Bean Soup, it is ground and combined with pickle relish for sandwich filling.

162

The menu says, "To give the utmost natural flavor our food is prepared with simplicity." Dutch Kitchen broils a lot of steaks and grinds its own fillets daily. I can vouch for the goodness of a Hamburger cooked medium rare; and what's a hamburger or a steak without a salad? I like to compare blue cheese dressings, and Dutch Kitchen's will join my list of good ones. It's also tasty spread on crackers or stuffed in celery, and the recipe is for either use.

I looked at one of the former menus, which called Dutch Kitchen "a chop house of exceptional merit." I didn't, however, get to see a 1903 menu that was being framed to hang in the restaurant. It was found in an old house by a young couple, who brought it to Dutch Kitchen. When the Stahls asked what they'd take for it, they said, "How about a couple whiskey sours?"

Dutch Kitchen is located at 12 East Washington Street in Hagerstown. Lunch is served from 11:30 a.m. until 2:00 p.m., Monday through Friday. Dinner is served from 4:30 p.m. until 9:30 p.m., Monday through Saturday. For reservations (preferred) call (301) 739-2252.

DUTCH KITCHEN'S BLUE CHEESE DRESSING

8 ounces blue cheese
8 ounces cream cheese
3 tablespoons mayonnaise
1½ tablespoons French
   dressing

¼ teaspoon garlic juice
½ cup milk

Soften cheeses and mash together. Add other ingredients and blend. Keeps two weeks in refrigerator, but more milk will have to be added as needed for salad dressing consistency. Yields about 1 pint.

Note: To use blue cheese mixture as a spread for crackers or stuffing for celery, omit milk or add a little as needed for desired consistency.

DUTCH KITCHEN'S FRIED
COUNT OYSTER SANDWICH

1 egg	12 count oysters
2 cups milk	peanut oil
dash of salt	6 hamburger buns
2 cups medium cracker meal	cocktail sauce
(or more)	

In one bowl combine egg, milk and salt, and beat thoroughly. Place cracker meal in another bowl, and dip oysters in meal, egg mixture, and meal again. Lay coated oysters on a tray and refrigerate for 24 hours. Fry in peanut oil heated to 350 degrees. Toast buns. Serve 2 oysters on each bun, with cocktail sauce on the side. Serves 6.

DUTCH KITCHEN'S BEAN SOUP
WITH COUNTRY HAM

2 cups dried great northern beans	1 teaspoon garlic juice
	2 ounces tomato sauce
country ham hock(s)	
1/2 medium Spanish onion, chopped fine	

Soak beans overnight. Boil ham hock for several hours until liquid has reduced to 1 gallon of stock. Cut some ham from the bone and put back in stock with drained beans and other ingredients. Cook slowly for 3 hours. Serves 10.

DUTCH KITCHEN'S COUNTRY HAM SANDWICH

2 cups ground country ham	additional mayonnaise to
2 tablespoons mayonnaise	spread
1 1/2 to 2 tablespoons pickle relish	12 slices white bread

Mix ham with mayonnaise and relish. Spread additional mayonnaise on bread slices. Spread with ham mixture, and toast sandwiches. Serves 6.

BISTRO
Cumberland

BISTRO

Bankers' hours are ideal—everyone knows that (except those who've worked in a bank, as I have). But how would you like to keep the hours of a restaurateur? "Twelve to twelve is nice," said Bistro's manager, Bill Miller. Admittedly a night person, he doesn't "do breakfast"; but he was wide awake talking to my husband Gordon and me about recipes and old buildings.

This restaurant's history is characteristic in a town undergoing active urban renewal. Many of Cumberland's old buildings have been razed to clear the way for rebuilding. Two years after moving into and redecorating their first location, Bistro was forced to move again when that building was slated for demolition. Their current location was headed for the same fate until Bistro purchased it.

The narrow, three-story facade of dark brick with sophisticated awnings over its doors has an appeal that's international. A gourmet shop on the first floor sells specialty foods, wines, imported cheeses, coffees and teas. The building is remembered as being an ice cream factory and a flower shop, both pleasant associations for a restaurant.

At Bistro, you can dine à la carte or select the fixed-price Gourmet Dinner. A typical gourmet menu might be a cup of Gumbo, Leeks Vinaigrette, Redfish Bienville, Bread Pudding or Bananas Foster and a glass of Muscadet. Or with twenty-four hours' notice you might order French Service for Two: King Crab Normandie or Chateaubriand.

Travelers like Gordon and myself rarely know where we'll be in twenty-four hours, so we made à la carte selections. A beefy Onion Soup Bistro flavored with sherry began our meal, along with crisp, seeded breadsticks and a cheese ball rolled in parsley. As an entrée, we selected Calves Liver with Wine Sauce. I'm a Southerner with a taste for liver served on grits with bacon and onions—but I found Bistro's delicate flambéed creation, served on rice with red and green peppers, to be a good diversion.

We also enjoyed Beef and Mushrooms Andrea, a casserole that's popular for lunch or a light evening meal. A mixture of

166

sour cream and Teriyaki sauce makes this dish similar to a stroganoff.

Lunch is served in the lounge on the first floor, behind the gourmet shop, past attractive walls of "recycled" wood from local barns. Sculpture, stained glass and paintings reflect the tastes of Bistro's owners, a physician and his decorator wife. Those tastes are apparent upstairs, too, in dining rooms named Imari, Rose Medallion, Victorian and the Garden Room, where draperies and china patterns are changed from winter to summer. Pick your surroundings and arrange a party.

Bistro is located at 37 North Centre Street in Cumberland. Lunch is served from 11:15 a.m. until 2:30 p.m., and dinner is served from 6:00 p.m. until 10:30 p.m., Monday through Saturday. For reservations (preferred) call (301) 777-8462.

BISTRO'S ONION SOUP BISTRO

2 tablespoons butter
1/4 cup oil
3 large onions, sliced
2 tablespoons flour
3 ounces beef bouillon (22 cubes)
1/2 ounce chicken base
2 cups straight sherry
1/4 pound (1 stick) butter
10 slices day-old French bread
1 pound Swiss cheese

In a heavy saucepan melt 2 tablespoons butter and add oil; sauté onions until they are transparent. Stir in flour, then add bouillon, chicken base and sherry. Cover and simmer for 30 minutes. To make croutons, melt 1/4 pound butter (or less) in a heavy skillet and brown both sides of French bread in butter. Ladle soup into bowls. Place one crouton in each bowl and top with 3 half-slices of cheese. Bake in a 350-degree oven for 15 minutes. Serves 10.

Note: For best flavor, refrigerate for 24 hours after simmering; reheat, add croutons and cheese, bake and serve.

BISTRO'S BEEF AND MUSHROOMS ANDREA

Andrea Sauce:

1 cup sour cream   ¼ cup Teriyaki sauce

Combine and keep at room temperature.

1 pound beef fillet tips   3 slices day-old French
5 tablespoons butter   bread
½ pound mushrooms, sliced

Sauté beef tips to desired doneness in 2 tablespoons butter. In another pan sauté mushrooms in 2 tablespoons butter. Keep beef and mushrooms warm. Brown both sides of French bread in 1 tablespoon butter (or more) to make croutons. Lay croutons in bottom of 3 individual casseroles. Mix beef and mushrooms, and put one-third of mixture on top of each crouton. Then spoon one-third of the Andrea Sauce over each casserole. Serves 3.

BISTRO'S CALVES LIVER WITH WINE SAUCE

2 slices calves liver (5- to   ¼ cup sliced green pepper
    6- ounce portions)   ¼ cup sliced red pepper
flour for dredging   1 ounce brandy
3 tablespoons butter   4 ounces consommé
¼ cup sliced onions   cooked rice for 2

Dredge calves liver in flour, and sauté to desired doneness in 2 tablespoons butter. Remove to heated platter. Add 1 tablespoon butter, onion and peppers to pan, and sauté until lightly done (peppers should retain their color, but lose crunchiness). Add brandy and ignite. Simmer until reduced by half. Add consommé, and reduce over increased heat until slightly thickened. Pour sauce over liver. Serve on rice. Serves 2.

L'OSTERIA
Cumberland

L'OSTERIA

I've been told that what makes a party is not the menu, but the men you sit beside. During my visit to L'Osteria, my attention was drawn to a bearded young man who sat by me at the next table. With him was a little girl, proudly swinging a purse. The man explained the menu to the child, mentioned something they ate at home, and ordered a drink for her, wine for himself. When she offered a toast to Mommie, it occurred to me that her mother was the chef. What a role model for a five-year-old!

That chef, wearing a white hat almost as tall as she was, had come to our table earlier to suggest that Gordon and I order one entrée that was a regular menu item (Pollo alla Romana) and one that was a daily special not on the menu (Bay Scallops Sienna). We said we'd also like to sample Veal Maria, the dish created in honor of Vincent Price by restaurateur Maria, who with her husband owns the restaurant and has a hand in the cooking.

Maria lets you know with flashing eyes and lilting voice that the cuisine at L'Osteria is authentic Northern Italian. She comes from Bologna and loves to cook. She made me feel like a guest in her own home, where, as hostess, she was overseeing a competent chef's preparation of my meal.

As we looked (and listened) and sipped Chianti, we also tasted the Insalata de Casa. The sight of that oil-and-vinegar-dressed house salad, with radishes and cherry tomatoes perfectly lined up on the smallest of Romaine leaves, made me imagine a sign on the kitchen door reading, "Artists at Work." Whatever artistic hands arranged the salad probably also fixed the Veal Maria. The plate was dressed up with bits of carrot-orange, parsley-green, and a lemon butterfly. (These garnishes aren't in the recipe, but you can add your own touch to make it pretty.) The chicken was also colorful, with pepper, onion and tomato, and the Bay Scallops Sienna even had color in its name. All three dishes proved as good to taste as to look at.

L'Osteria is part of Colonial Manor, a motel with a past. Originally called Turkey Flight Manor, the building has a strong association with the Civil War. Having housed wounded soldiers on its top floor, the building itself was wounded by a cannonball during a battle at nearby Flock's Mill. Walls in the attic still show scribbled reminders that soldiers were there. One Union soldier drew large sketches of two generals who were captured in Cumberland in 1865 by McNeill's Raiders. I wonder whether Vincent Price critiqued that art when he visited L'Osteria.

L'Osteria is located at Colonial Manor Motel, Route 40, one mile east of Cumberland. Dinner is served from 6:00 p.m. until 10:00 p.m., Monday through Saturday. Brunch is served from 11:30 a.m. until 2:00 p.m. on Sunday. For reservations (recommended) call (301) 777-3553.

L'OSTERIA'S BAY SCALLOPS SIENNA

1 pound fresh bay scallops
$\frac{1}{2}$ cup dry white wine
1 cup Marinara Sauce (see note on next page)

$\frac{1}{2}$ cup sour cream
salt and pepper
$\frac{1}{2}$ pound pasta (your choice)

Wash and drain scallops, then poach in wine until white. Add Marinara Sauce. Turn off heat and gently blend in sour cream. Season with salt and pepper to taste, and serve over hot cooked pasta. Serves 4.

L'OSTERIA'S VEAL MARIA

1 pound veal scallops
flour to coat veal
$\frac{1}{4}$ pound butter
$\frac{3}{4}$ cup marinated mushrooms

$\frac{3}{4}$ cup marinated artichoke hearts
salt and pepper
$\frac{1}{2}$ pound pasta (your choice)

Pound veal scallops as thin as possible, and dredge lightly in flour. Sauté veal in butter until meat juices are yellow, *not pink*. Add marinated mushrooms and artichoke hearts, and heat through. Season with salt and pepper to taste, and serve over hot cooked pasta. Serves 4.

171

L'OSTERIA'S POLLO ALLA ROMANA

olive oil to coat skillet

4 whole chicken breasts,
  boned, cut into strips

1 large green pepper, sliced
  into strips

1 large onion, sliced into
  thick strips

½ cup white wine

1 cup Marinara Sauce (see
  note)

salt and pepper

½ pound pasta (your choice)

Heat olive oil in a large skillet. Add chicken strips and cook until white, turning frequently to prevent sticking. Add green pepper and onion and sauté until tender. Deglaze skillet with white wine. Add Marinara Sauce and heat through. Season with salt and pepper to taste, and serve over hot cooked pasta. Serves 4.

Note: See index for Marinara Sauce, or use 1 cup of chopped, canned tomatoes and their juice, seasoned with sweet basil and oregano to your taste. Heat through to develop flavor.

FRED WARNER'S GERMAN RESTAURANT
Cresaptown

**FRED WARNER'S
RESTAURANT**

During President John F. Kennedy's administration, a taxi arrived at Fred Warner's German Restaurant one day to pick up two "Bee Sting" Cakes. They were then transported by airplane and helicopter to the White House. Few people get that kind of delivery service, but the Bienstich or "Bee Sting" Cakes are very popular at Fred Warner's. "The people like them gooey," Warner says, so he puts in lots of honey, rum and black walnuts. Also justly famous are his Apple Strudels and loaves of fresh-baked Rye Bread.

The rye flour used for the bread comes from the 1877 gristmill that Fred Warner, Sr., used to operate in West Virginia. And on the rye bread go slices of ham cooked the way Fred's father did it: baked with rings of pineapple, maraschino cherries and sweet, spicy cloves. So ham on rye says something special at Fred Warner's—something about the value of family and carrying on traditions.

"Mountain people are my kind of people," Fred said as he described the German valley in West Virginia where his mother's home, a log house with a tin roof, was built during the Civil War. He named a creamy yellow salad dressing "Hansel Mountain Mamma Dressing" for his mountain mamma and his brother Hansel, who also worked in the gristmill. When the mill was sold in 1928, the Warners built the building in Cresaptown that was first a grocery store and is now Fred Warner's German Restaurant.

The restaurant is intimate and informal. "Willkommen" is spoken here in an arborlike dining room where bunches of grapes hang from the ceiling. Gordon and I were at Fred Warner's for lunch, and we sampled salad bar offerings spread over several checked tablecloths. We could easily have made a meal just from cold Potato Salad, Cheese Bread, and Apple Butter. I tried several different dressings over bits of spinach and lettuce, and naturally my favorite was Hansel Mountain Mamma. It was oniony and sweet.

While we ate our salads, Fred Warner and his wife Marian brought a bottle of May wine to our table with the best

Wiener Schnitzel I have ever eaten. The secret seems to be in grinding the veal cutlets very fine and coating them with crumbs processed from homemade bread. With the veal we ate crunchy Potato Pancakes, Sauerkraut and cold Apfelmus (applesauce). I like sauerkraut even straight from a can; but when it's cooked with pork ribs and apples, it earns its reputation as a good German vegetable.

It was a "glorious evening," Fred said, when forty-seven Germans on business in this country came to the restaurant, starved for a good German dinner. They listened to country and western music while they ate, and later they wrote to say it was a highlight of their itinerary. A highlight of *your* trip to Maryland might be one of four yearly festivals at Fred Warner's, with bite-sized desserts and general feasting, dancing and German bands from Washington. Wunderbar!

Fred Warner's German Restaurant is located on Route 220 South in Cresaptown. Meals are served from 11:00 a.m. until 11:00 p.m., Tuesday through Saturday, and from noon until 8:00 p.m. on Sunday. For reservations (accepted, but not necessary) call (301) 729-2361.

FRED WARNER'S GERMAN RESTAURANT'S
APPLE STRUDEL

Dough:

½ tablespoon butter, melted   ½ cup warm water
1 egg, beaten   2 cups all-purpose flour

Mix together butter, egg and water. Work in enough flour to make a soft dough. Make into a small round loaf, place it on a plate and cover with waxed paper to rest for 30 minutes.

Filling:

5 cups sliced apples   ½ teaspoon cinnamon
½ cup brown sugar   ½ cup raisins
2 tablespoons butter

Put a large cloth on a flat surface and sprinkle flour on the cloth. Stretch dough on the cloth until it is very thin. Spread

175

apples on dough. Sprinkle with brown sugar, cinnamon and raisins, and dot with butter. Using edge of cloth, roll up dough like a jelly roll. Place in a lightly greased, long pan (9x13 inches) and bake in a 350-degree oven for 30 minutes. Ladle juices over strudel. Bake another 30 minutes, and ladle again. Bake an additional 30 minutes (a total of 1½ hours) and remove from oven. Ladle juices over golden brown strudel, and serve warm with cream, ice cream or whipped cream. Serves 8.

FRED WARNER'S GERMAN RESTAURANT'S HANSEL MOUNTAIN MAMMA DRESSING

1 cup peanut oil
½ small onion, cut in
  chunks
1 cup sugar
¾ teaspoon prepared
  mustard

¼ teaspoon salt
½ cup white salad vinegar
½ teaspoon lemon juice

Put first five ingredients in blender jar and mix on high speed for 2 minutes. Add vinegar and lemon juice and blend for a few seconds. Serve on sliced tomatoes, tossed salad, or spinach or other greens. Yields 1 pint.

FRED WARNER'S GERMAN RESTAURANT'S SAUERKRAUT

1 pound pork ribs
2 28-ounce cans sauerkraut,
  drained and rinsed
¼ cup sugar

¼ small onion, diced
½ teaspoon caraway seeds
1 unpeeled Red Delicious
  apple, finely chopped

Cover pork ribs with water and cook until tender. Remove ribs from broth, pick off lean meat and return meat to broth. Add sauerkraut. Add remaining ingredients, cover and simmer for about 1½ hours. Serves 8.

AU PETIT PARIS
Frostburg

AU PETIT PARIS   A little bit of Paris is not what one would expect to find on U. S. 40 in Western Maryland, but it's been there for twenty-five years. It's a "special occasion" place for local diners—a woman outside the Public Library next door told me she thinks of it for a graduation treat or an anniversary party. But it is also a place for businessmen entertaining clients, or for travelers looking for authentic French food.

The authenticity comes from the St. Marie family, who own and operate Au Petit Paris. The father (chef), mother (hostess), son (waiter) and daughter (bartender) do their jobs with polished efficiency.

For most of its years, the building (which was burned and rebuilt in the 1880s) was a furniture store. Deliveries were made by horse and wagon down the alley that is now the entrance to Au Petit Paris. Guests enter a courtyard through a canopied door that separates Main Street from the experience of French dining.

Gordon and I found the whole meal, from frothy Creme Vichyssoise through Mousse au Chocolat Avec Grand Marnier, to be a special occasion. The bowls of Vichyssoise were nestled in deep crystal plates of ice, with parsley garnishing both the ice and the delicately seasoned soup. The Mousse, with the distinctive taste of Grand Marnier, was topped with whipped cream and chocolate dots. I should tell you that we couldn't resist also dividing a slice of fresh, delicious Raspberry Cream Cake.

It was amazing that we ever reached dessert, having stuffed ourselves with entrées of Roti de Porc and Coq au Vin. Now I have authentic French recipes for rolled pork roast and—how do you say *Coq au Vin* in English? Of course, appetites grow on the strength of such good cooking, and ours were also enhanced by a Louis Martini Pinot Noir.

Do you wonder, as I did, how the St. Maries happened to come to Frostburg? Au Petit Paris was begun as a club in Amarillo, Texas, for off-duty French air force personnel assigned to the jet aircraft school there. After Louis St. Marie left the air force and the school, he and his wife developed Au Petit Paris into a commercial restaurant and continued to operate it in Texas until 1959. Then they were approached by a citizen of Frostburg, whose wife owned a dress shop in the building on Main Street. The St. Maries were invited to move Au Petit Paris to Frostburg, and they thought it was a good idea. Now, as their motto states, they are "Serving The World From Western Maryland."

Au Petit Paris is located at 86 East Main Street in Frostburg. Dinner is served from 6:00 p.m. until 9:30 p.m., Tuesday through Saturday. For reservations (required) call (301) 689-8946.

AU PETIT PARIS'S COQ AU VIN

1 whole chicken breast, split
2 chicken legs
salt and pepper
flour for dredging
6 to 8 pearl onions, peeled
6 fresh mushrooms, sliced
2 to 3 tablespoons clarified butter

1 tablespoon olive oil
1 garlic clove, mashed
2 tablespoons brandy
¾ cup chicken stock
1¾ cups Burgundy wine
2 sprigs parsley

Pat all the chicken parts dry, season them with salt and pepper, dredge them in flour and set aside. In a large skillet over moderate heat, sauté onions and mushrooms in 1 to 2 tablespoons of clarified butter, turning vegetables frequently until lightly brown. Set vegetables aside, leaving butter in pan. Add olive oil to pan, along with more butter if needed and half the garlic clove. Add chicken, skin side down, and sauté for 12 to 15 minutes or until chicken is lightly browned. Turn chicken and repeat. Remove chicken and drain excess fat from pan. Return chicken to pan, add brandy and flame, turning the chicken. When flame has died out, add chicken stock and wine, the remaining half of the garlic clove, the parsley, onions and mushrooms. Bring to a quick simmer.

179

With a wooden spoon, scrape residue from bottom of pan and stir into the stock. Transfer everything to a casserole. Cover and place in a moderate (350-degree) oven for 30 minutes or until chicken is tender. Remove chicken from casserole; set on a platter and keep warm. Strain liquid and bring it to a boil, stirring until it has the consistency of heavy cream. Pour over chicken. Serves 2.

AU PETIT PARIS'S ROTI DE PORC

1 3½- to 4-pound boneless loin of pork, rolled and tied
3 cups water
1 cup dry white wine
2 stalks celery, cut in chunks
2 medium carrots, cut in chunks
1 medium onion, cut in chunks

3 to 4 sprigs parsley
1 bay leaf
salt and pepper to taste
2 cups brown sauce (commercial or homemade)
¾ cup Madeira wine
½ cup raisins
2 tart apples, peeled, cored and sliced thin

Place the roast in a pan and add the water, white wine, celery, carrots, onion, parsley and bay leaf. Season the roast with salt and pepper, and cover it with foil, sealing it tight around the edges. Place in a 400-degree oven for about 45 minutes. Remove foil and insert meat thermometer, placing probe in center of roast. Lower the heat to 350 degrees and continue to cook, uncovered, basting the roast every 15 minutes, until thermometer indicates well done. Remove roast from oven and place on a serving platter; keep warm. Strain liquid from roasting pan into a saucepan. Remove as much grease as possible. Reduce the stock by half over moderate heat. Add brown sauce, Madeira wine, raisins and apple slices. Slice pork roast and serve the sauce in a sauceboat or top each slice with the sauce. Serves 6 to 8.

THE CASSELMAN
Grantsville

THE CASSELMAN

Parents, listen to your children. When thirteen-year-old Philip Miller saw a "For Sale" sign on the lawn of the old Casselman Hotel in 1964, he told his parents about the opportunity. The Ivan Millers, Mennonite farmers, were amused by their son's enthusiasm, but they investigated and decided to buy the property that an ancestor had owned almost a century earlier. With hard work and the common sense that comes from raising ten children, the Millers eventually developed the old hotel into an incorporated family business. They built a modern kitchen and reopened the Casselman's restaurant, which had been closed for twenty years; then they added a bakery and built a forty-room motor inn behind the hotel.

This Federal-style structure, built of handmade bricks fired on the site, has gone by many names: Sterner's Tavern, Drover's Inn, Farmer's Hotel and Dorsey's Hotel. It was built in 1824 to accommodate travelers on the Old National Road, now part of U.S. 40. Nowhere in my travels of that long highway have I been more impressed by its place in history than in Grantsville.

The road was first an Indian trail for pack horses and was called Nemacolin's Path. Later it aided the military as a supply line and was named Braddock's Road for the general who had it widened from six to twelve feet. It was called the Cumberland Road after Congress appropriated funds in 1806 to rebuild it from Cumberland, Maryland, to Wheeling, West Virginia—making it the first national highway.

When that same road brought Gordon and me to Grantsville, The Casselman's Dorsey Room was ready for us. We went right to sleep in a carved antique bed. I dreamed—or did I?—that someone slipped down the hall in the wee hours to start breakfast, and soon bakery smells wafted upstairs.

Those smells called us to breakfast in a dining room appropriately wallpapered with road scenes. The souvenir placemat that announced "Rooms & Meals in a Quiet Country Atmosphere" gave equal space to facts about The Casselman and the Old National Road.

182

Gordon began the day with Oatmeal served with a dish of brown sugar. I was tempted by the peanut butter and jelly offered as an extra with an English Muffin, but I passed that up for one of the Cinnamon Buns that I smelled baking.

When I visited the bakery, which is in the basement with a gift shop, I saw their popular Applesauce Nut Bread being made for takeout orders as well as for use in the dining room. It's the fruity, nutty, spicy kind of bread that is as welcome as cake at our house.

The Casselman's cuisine is simple and substantial country food with a variety of favorite Amish recipes. Before leaving, we sampled two of the dishes prepared for lunch, Baked Beans and the ever-popular Shoofly Pie. The beans, baked with a tasty amount of catsup and brown sugar, seemed like a good dish to take to a church supper. The Casselman's Shoofly Pie calls for a filling of light and dark syrup rather than cane molasses—another of many variations on the most famous Amish recipe of all.

The Casselman is located on Main Street in Grantsville. Meals are served from 7:00 a.m. until 8:00 p.m., Monday through Thursday, and from 7:00 a.m. until 9:00 p.m. (10:00 p.m. in the summer) on Friday and Saturday. For reservations (necessary for parties of 6 or more) call (301) 895-5266.

THE CASSELMAN'S BAKED BEANS

2 cups navy (or great
  northern) dried beans
1/2 cup brown sugar
1/4 cup catsup
1/2 small onion, finely
  chopped

1/8 teaspoon dry mustard
pinch of ginger
1/2 cup chopped ham or
  bacon bits
1 12-ounce can tomato juice

Soak beans in cold water for several hours or overnight; then cook until beans are almost soft. Add remaining ingredients (tomato juice should cover mixture), and bake in a 3-quart casserole or baking pan in a 325-degree oven for 45 minutes. Serves 8.

THE CASSELMAN'S SHOOFLY PIE

Filling:

1/2 teaspoon baking soda
3/4 cup boiling water
1/2 cup dark corn syrup

1/2 cup light corn syrup
1 9-inch pie shell, unbaked

Dissolve soda in boiling water, then add syrups. Cool, then pour into pie shell.

Topping:

1 cup flour
1/2 cup brown sugar

1/2 teaspoon baking soda
1/4 cup shortening

Combine flour, sugar and soda. Using your fingers, rub shortening into flour mixture until crumbly. Spoon over filling. Bake pie in a 375-degree oven for approximately 35 minutes. Yields 1 pie.

THE CASSELMAN'S APPLESAUCE NUT BREAD

2 eggs, slightly beaten
1 1/4 cups applesauce
3 tablespoons cooking oil
3/4 cup sugar
3/4 cup chopped nuts
2 cups all-purpose flour

1 tablespoon baking powder
1 teaspoon salt
1/2 teaspoon baking soda
3/4 teaspoon cinnamon
1/2 teaspoon cloves

Combine ingredients in order given. Mix, but do not overbeat. Pour into greased bread pan, and bake at 375 degrees for 1 hour or until tester comes out clean. Yields one 1-pound loaf.

PENN ALPS RESTAURANT
Grantsville

PENN ALPS RESTAURANT

Sometime in the 1830s, keepers of the Inn at Little Crossings (later Dixie Tavern and now Penn Alps) got word from a stagecoach company to have plenty of beef and boiled potatoes ready at a certain time. Thirty prominent Indians, on their way to see President Andrew Jackson, would stop there for dinner. The inn also prepared turkeys for a party of white people due at the same time, but their coach ran late and couldn't stop; so the Indians feasted on both meats. What they ate at the inn on their way home is not recorded, but what they wore is interesting. The men had on broadcloth suits, and the one squaw wore a beaded dress—quite a contrast to the blankets they'd worn to Washington.

In the old log stagecoach stop, constructed in 1818 and since remodeled, Penn Alps Restaurant and Craft Shop serves meals and shows such crafts as weaving, ceramics and woodcarving—both the method and the finished product. The craft program helps the people of Upper Appalachia market their handiwork and makes their customers more aware of art processes. The day Gordon and I were there, a craftsman was carving birds so real we had to feel their feathers. He worked in one of several log cabins across from the main building while visitors strolled in to watch him.

Our walking tour also took in the Casselman River Bridge, the largest stone arch in America when it was built in 1813. George Washington forded the Casselman River in 1755 and named the area The Little Crossings.

The founder of Penn Alps, Dr. Alta Schrock, pushed aside plants and books to get to my questions. She was preparing a nutrition lecture, she said, but "the Lord will help me put it together." I had the feeling that that had been her approach when she bought the place in 1959 and started a restaurant. She called in a woman from the kitchen to ask her about a recipe and introduced her warmly with, "I found her in a corn patch twenty-four years ago."

Gordon and I browsed in the craft shop while those from a touring bus ate lunch. I was attracted to a pink chintz

186

chicken with red felt comb and brown rickrack braid. It was priced as reasonably as chickens I buy at the grocery store. I tucked it under my arm to add to my craft collection, while Penn Alps Restaurant's Chicken Stuffing was added to my recipe collection.

Most of the recipes used at Penn Alps are Pennsylvania Dutch, the local term for foods originating in southern Germany. I asked how to prepare a favorite Penn Dutch vegetable, dried corn, thinking of some friends who have corn drying in their solar-heated greenhouse. Penn Alps uses a ton of dried corn a year, either cooking it in the restaurant or selling it by the pound in the craft shop.

For our late lunch at Penn Alps, Gordon and I ate a hearty German Vegetable Soup, crisp Coleslaw and Applesauce spiced with cinnamon. A waitress said their most popular dessert was Bob Andy Pie, and we went with the crowd. It reminded me of my favorite chess pie, but it was spicier and cooked with milk. No one could answer my question: who were Bob and Andy?

Penn Alps Restaurant is located on U.S. 40 in Grantsville. Meals are served from 11:00 a.m. until 7:00 p.m., Monday through Thursday, and from 8:00 a.m. until 8:00 p.m., Friday and Saturday, November through April. Meals are served from 8:00 a.m. until 8:00 p.m., Monday through Saturday, May through October. Reservations are not required, but the phone number is (301) 895-5985.

PENN ALPS RESTAURANT'S DRIED CORN

1 cup dried corn	1 tablespoon sugar
6 cups water	4 tablespoons margarine
1/2 teaspoon salt	1/3 cup half and half

Simmer the corn in water for 1 hour to reconstitute it. After it has cooked, add salt, sugar and margarine. Add half and half, stir until thoroughly heated, and serve. Serves 4.

187

PENN ALPS RESTAURANT'S BOB ANDY PIE

2/3 cup butter
1½ cups sugar
3 tablespoons flour
4 egg yolks, beaten
1 tablespoon cloves

1 tablespoon cinnamon
4 egg whites, beaten until
  stiff
3 cups milk, scalded
2 unbaked 9-inch pie crusts

Combine butter, sugar, flour, egg yolks, cloves and cinnamon; mix well. Blend in egg whites. Add milk to the mixture, stir well and pour into pie crusts. Bake at 350 degrees for 45 minutes or until set. Yields two 9-inch pies.

PENN ALPS RESTAURANT'S CHICKEN STUFFING

1 pound loaf bread
2 tablespoons butter
3 ribs celery, diced
1 onion, diced
½ teaspoon black pepper
¾ teaspoon poultry
  seasoning

2 cups chicken broth
3 eggs
½ cup ham, diced
½ cup American cheese,
  diced

Leaving crusts on the bread, cut it into cubes and set aside. Melt the butter in a skillet. Add celery and onion and sauté until soft. Add pepper and poultry seasoning while cooking. Add the celery and onion mixture and the chicken broth to the bread. Beat eggs in a separate bowl and add to bread (mixture should be wet). Add ham and cheese to bread mixture. Combine well. Yields enough to stuff two 5-pound chickens or one turkey.

Note: Stuffing can also be baked in a 9x13-inch pan.

CORNISH MANOR
Oakland

CORNISH MANOR

"**I**f ever you had a thought to buy a country home, it would be wise to SEE THIS," said the elaborate real estate brochure. In addition to an eighteen-room house on twenty acres referred to as "the most beautiful tract in Garrett County," this estate had crystal-pure water piped from town, electric lights and a Bell telephone. Built in 1868 by a judge from Washington, the summer house was sold by its second owner when poor health required him to move to the city. At that time the estate was called Ethelhurst, named for the owner's daughter Ethel. Later owners gave it their name, Cornish, which the present owners kept for the restaurant, Cornish Manor.

We ate in the sun parlor on the front of the house, an enclosed portion of the 125-foot-long veranda. The bar is located in this room, which is popular whether the sun or the moon is shining through its bank of windows.

Owner Bob Bobo, who's been there twenty years, showed Gordon how to make a drink he called a Brown Bear. I wondered if Bob had seen too many Brown Bears himself when he described visits he'd had with Tom, the Cornish Manor ghost. I asked how he knew the ghost's name was Tom. Bob answered, "He told me it was." When Patty Bobo added that the ghost "has Elizabeth Taylor eyes," I was intrigued. She enlarged upon her husband's story: Tom is a "good" rascal with a goatee, and he dresses like a sea captain. A longtime waitress at Cornish Manor told me about the time a child, dining with his family in a back room, kept looking at the staircase and asking about the man on the steps (whom no one else could see). I didn't have the pleasure of meeting Tom, but I did sample a Brown Bear. The milkshake look-alike is a blend of several liqueurs and cream, served in a champagne glass.

In the wide front hall a blackboard lists luncheon specials. Some people come on a certain day for Chicken and Dumplings. I would have liked that, too, but I'm glad I didn't miss Crab à la Maryland. It was something like my favorite Chicken à la King, with mushrooms and a good flavor of

190

sherry. Other diners beat us to Sweet and Sour Spinach, the fresh vegetable of the day, and ate it all up. I'd like to try that next time, as well as the popular Barley Soup.

Bob Bobo insisted that we taste the dessert with the house name, Cornish Pudding, which I found would satisfy any sweet tooth. This pudding cake forms its own crust as it bakes; then it is served over ice cream.

After lunch, our hosts invited us upstairs to see their spacious living quarters. Then we walked in the yard, now reduced to seven acres, and toured the cave behind the house. Cornish Manor uses it for cold storage of food, but Bob Bobo dreams of having a bar out there. He'd hate to lose the storage space, but that cave would be the perfect place for a Brown Bear.

Cornish Manor is located on Memorial Drive (the old Deer Park Road) in Oakland. Lunch is served from 11:00 a.m. until 4:00 p.m., and dinner is from 4:00 p.m. until 10:00 p.m., Monday through Saturday. For reservations (accepted) call (301) 334-3551.

CORNISH MANOR'S CORNISH PUDDING

3½ cups brown sugar	1 teaspoon cinnamon
3 cups water	1½ cups flour
3 tablespoons maple syrup	½ cup raisins
⅓ cup butter	milk (approximately ½ cup)
3 teaspoons baking powder	ice cream
1 teaspoon nutmeg	whipped cream and cherries

Combine 3 cups of the brown sugar with the water and the maple syrup; heat through and set aside. Cream remaining ½ cup brown sugar with butter. Sift together dry ingredients and add along with the raisins. Then add just enough milk to make consistency of thick cake batter. Pour syrup into a 3-quart baking dish, and drop batter by spoonfuls into syrup. Bake in a 400-degree oven for 25 minutes or until brown. Serve over ice cream, and top with whipped cream and a cherry. Serves 8.

191

CORNISH MANOR'S CRAB A LA MARYLAND

¼ cup margarine
½ cup canned chopped
  mushrooms, drained
1 tablespoon finely chopped
  onion
1 pound crabmeat, picked
¾ teaspoon Worcestershire
  sauce

¼ cup dry sherry
1 cup milk
3 tablespoons flour
salt and pepper
4 slices Swiss cheese

Melt margarine in a large iron skillet. Add mushrooms and onions and sauté until tender; do *not* brown. Add crabmeat, Worcestershire sauce and sherry. In a mixing bowl, make a paste of milk and flour. Add to crabmeat mixture and cook until thick. Add salt and pepper to taste. Place in 4 individual casseroles, top each with a slice of cheese and broil until cheese melts. Serves 4.

CORNISH MANOR'S BROWN BEAR

¾ ounce dark Creme de
  Cacao
¾ ounce Kahlúa
¼ ounce white Creme de
  Menthe

¼ ounce Tia Maria
1 ounce coffee cream
1 ounce whipped cream

Shake all ingredients with ice, then strain into a champagne glass. Serves 1.

PC'S 1897 SALOON & EATERY
Oakland

PC'S 1897 SALOON & EATERY

In PC's dining room one evening, a party commented on the realistic train sounds in the background. They thought they were hearing a nostalgic recording, not knowing that had they stepped out the back door (as we did) they would have been almost on the main line tracks of the B. & O. Railroad. The tracks are within twenty feet of the building, and about a dozen freight trains pass each day, mostly carrying coal.

Having worked on the railroad in our early careers, Gordon and I were glad that a train rumbled by while we were there. We found it exciting to step out the kitchen door and onto creosoted crossties. Looking down the curved track, we saw the depot and the train signal showing "high green," meaning the track was clear.

The railroad had a lot to do with developing a resort clientele for Oakland and for Garrett County, which was named for John W. Garrett, president of the Baltimore and Ohio Railroad at the time of the county's creation in 1872. Tourists still stop at the Queen Anne–style railroad station near PC's—not passengers, but photographers hoping to capture the 1884 building on film.

Another attraction for today's tourists is Garrett County skiing, as wintertime visitors to PC's 1897 Saloon and Eatery will tell you. Skiers are attracted to PC's by the thought of a warming drink at the bar or a meal in front of one of the largest fireplaces in Maryland.

The 1897 building that houses PC's was partially burned in a 1940s fire. All that remains of the original saloon room is the tin ceiling. The dining room, however, still has its original maple floorboards—the widest is twenty-five inches. Hand-hewn beams in the ceiling halted railroad traffic for two hours when they were moved across the tracks.

The dining room is furnished with antique reproductions and lighted with Tiffany-style lamps made by local artists. An old sewing machine at the entrance holds menus and announcements of specials. Several times a week the chef introduces something unusual, such as Fresh Rabbit, Catfish or Frog Legs.

Gordon and I ate in the dining room on a day too hot for a fire. We began our meal with Curried Apple Wedges, which were sautéed in butter with brown sugar and curry, then wrapped in bacon and broiled. I might have been tempted by the Shrimp Creole had the weather been cooler, but we tried the recommended Frog Legs Forestière and found them cooked to perfection.

Carlo Rossi wines are served by the glass, but I had a California Cooler, a refreshing combination of white wine and four fruit juices. Then I dreamed of hopping a fast freight west.

PC's 1897 Saloon & Eatery is located at 123 South Second Street in Oakland. Meals are served from 11:00 a.m. until 11:00 p.m., Monday through Saturday. For reservations (preferred for large groups) call (301) 334-1611.

PC's 1897 SALOON & EATERY'S
FROG LEGS FORESTIERE

4 pairs frog legs	**1 ounce brandy**
flour for dusting	**cooked rice for 2**
¼ pound butter	**2 lemon wedges**
4 ounces onion, chopped	
4 ounces mushrooms,	
chopped	

Dust frog legs with flour. Melt butter in a skillet over moderate heat and panfry frog legs with onion and mushrooms until opaque. Add brandy and deglaze skillet. Simmer for one minute. Place frog legs on bed of rice and cover with sauce. Garnish with lemon wedges. Serves 2.

PC'S 1897 SALOON & EATERY'S
CURRIED APPLE WEDGES

2 firm apples	**2 teaspoons curry powder**
2 tablespoons butter	**16 slices bacon**
2 tablespoons brown sugar	

Core apples and divide each into 8 wedges, leaving skin on. In a skillet melt butter and add brown sugar and curry. Quickly sauté apples in curry mixture. When apple wedges have cooled, wrap each one in a slice of raw bacon. Place on a baking sheet and broil until bacon is done. Yields 4 appetizer servings.

PC'S 1897 SALOON & EATERY'S SHRIMP CREOLE

3 tablespoons salad oil
½ cup chopped onion
½ cup chopped celery
1 garlic clove, minced
2 cups canned tomatoes
1 8-ounce can seasoned
  tomato sauce
1 ½ teaspoons salt
1 teaspoon sugar
½ teaspoon chili powder

1 tablespoon Worcestershire
  sauce
dash of Tabasco sauce
1 teaspoon cornstarch
2 teaspoons water
12 ounces raw shrimp,
  cleaned
½ cup chopped green
  pepper
cooked rice for 6

Heat oil in a skillet. Sauté onion, celery and garlic until tender but not brown. Add tomatoes, tomato sauce and seasonings. Simmer, uncovered, for 45 minutes. Mix cornstarch with 2 teaspoons water, and stir into sauce. Cook, stirring, until mixture thickens. Add shrimp and green pepper. Cover and simmer until done, about 5 minutes. Serve over rice or in rice ring. Serves 5 to 6.

THE CHIMNEY CORNER
Red House

THE CHIMNEY CORNER

When the owner of The Chimney Corner says, "If these old walls could talk," she's referring to walls of solid chestnut logs, built in 1932. As soon as I saw those old logs, chinked inside and out with white cement, I understood why the restaurant is advertised as "clean." The white cement between dark logs has the fresh look that I remember from whitewashed tree trunks in my grandfather's front yard. White café curtains with tied-back cotton ruffles add to the "clean" look and complement the chestnut tables trimmed with silver birch. Accessories, too, are rustic wood. Hickory logs make stands that hold a guest book and the service trays.

A wagon bought from an Amish family was customized to hold a salad bar full of good things. After tasting the restaurant's Spaghetti Salad, which mixes salad vegetables with pasta rather than tossing them with lettuce, I asked for the recipe. I also got the recipe for the tomato-red Bean Soup often served with the salad bar.

Gordon and I arrived for breakfast, a good time to be at The Chimney Corner since it specializes in Hickory Smoked Hams, Baked Sausage and Buckwheat Cakes. Gordon, the pancake maker at our house, ordered the Raised Buckwheat Cakes that are served there about ten months of the year. (They sometimes run out of buckwheat flour and have to wait until autumn for a new supply.) The cakes were fluffy and had the good taste of yeast bread.

A basket of Pumpkin Bread, with the raisins still warm, accompanied our meal. Tasty at breakfast, the pretty, brown loaf could have been a nice dessert as well.

My first impressions at The Chimney Corner were of pink petunias in windowboxes and signs hanging above them: Buckwheat Flour and Hickory Smoked Hams. (Hams, Sausage and Liver Pudding can be purchased and shipped.)

The Chimney Corner is a forty- by eighty-foot building where people used to gather for square dances. (Alcohol might have been drunk there then, but it isn't now.) The chimney for which the restaurant is named is built of thirty-five tons of stone and has a fireplace on two sides. Even without a fire, we found it hospitable, with yellow cosmos and an old clock on the mantel. The chimney is a good backdrop for quilts and craft items sold in the corner of the room.

Although we had to make a special trip to get to the junction of Routes 219 and 50, the area used to be a stagecoach and wagon stop for people traveling over the Great Backbone Mountain to West Virginia. The crossroads village was named Red House simply because its first house, built in 1830, was painted red.

The Chimney Corner is located at the junction of U. S. Highways 50 and 219 at Red House. Meals are served from 6:00 a.m. until 8:00 p.m., Monday through Friday; and from 8:00 a.m. until 8:00 p.m., Saturday and Sunday. The restaurant is closed on Thanksgiving, Christmas and New Year's Day. Reservations are not necessary, but the phone number is (301) 334-2040.

THE CHIMNEY CORNER'S BEAN SOUP

3 cups great northern beans
1 carrot, diced
1 stalk celery, diced
1 cup cooked ham, diced
1 tablespoon garlic salt
1 tablespoon seasoned salt
7 ounces tomato catsup
1 48-ounce can vegetable
   cocktail juice

Soak beans overnight, then simmer them with carrot and celery until beans are tender. Do not drain. Add ham and remaining ingredients, and cook another 15 to 20 minutes. Serves 10.

THE CHIMNEY CORNER'S SPAGHETTI SALAD

1 8-ounce box spaghetti
2 tomatoes, diced
2 cucumbers, diced
1 large Bermuda onion,
   diced
1 large green pepper, diced
1 2³/₄-ounce bottle Salad
   Supreme spice blend
1 8-ounce bottle French
   dressing

Cook spaghetti according to package directions. Drain, rinse, and set aside to cool. In a large bowl, combine other ingredients. Add spaghetti; mix well. Refrigerate. Serves 8.

THE CHIMNEY CORNER'S PUMPKIN BREAD

1 cup cooking oil
3 eggs
3 cups sugar
3 cups cooked pumpkin
3 tablespoons vanilla
5 cups flour
1 teaspoon baking soda
1 teaspoon salt
1 teaspoon baking powder
1 teaspoon nutmeg
1 teaspoon cinnamon
$\frac{1}{2}$ cup nuts
$\frac{1}{2}$ cup raisins

Combine oil, eggs, sugar, pumpkin and vanilla, beating well. Mix the dry ingredients, nuts and raisins together and add to first mixture, blending well. Pour into two greased and floured 9x5x3-inch loaf pans, and bake at 325 degrees for 1¼ hours. Yields 2 loaves.

THE CHIMNEY CORNER'S
RAISED BUCKWHEAT CAKES

2 cups warm water
1 package dry yeast
$\frac{1}{2}$ tablespoon sugar
3 to 3½ cups (approximately 1 pound) buckwheat flour
$\frac{1}{2}$ cup buttermilk
1 tablespoon corn syrup
1 tablespoon brown sugar
$\frac{1}{2}$ teaspoon baking soda
$\frac{1}{2}$ teaspoon baking powder
$\frac{1}{2}$ teaspoon salt
$\frac{1}{2}$ cup hot water, approximately

In a large bowl mix warm water, yeast and sugar; then add enough buckwheat flour to make a very stiff batter. Let rise to top of bowl. Knead and let rise again. When you are ready to bake, add buttermilk and remaining ingredients. Stir in enough hot water to make a thin batter. Bake on a very hot griddle. Makes 15 to 18 pancakes.

Note: You may reserve enough batter, approximately ½ cup, to use as starter for next batch. Add it to yeast mixture with the flour before letting mixture rise.

INDEX

APPETIZERS
Blue Cheese Dressing-Spread, Dutch Kitchen 163
Clams Casino, Cockey's Tavern 128
Crab Balls, The Chambers 19
Curried Apple Wedges, PC's 195
Empanadas, The Treaty of Paris 64
Escargot au Moutarde, Country Fare Inn 112
Escargot in Mushroom Caps, The Inn at Perry Cabin 32
French-Fried Vegetables, Kitty Knight House 40
Mushroom Turnover, The Penwick House 67
Mussels Marinara, Fiori 115
Oysters à la Gino, Robert Morris Inn 24
Oysters Browne, Harry Browne's 48
Oysters Roberto, The Ott House 155
Pineapple Fritters, Blair Mansion Inn 72

BEVERAGES
Brown Bear, Cornish Manor 192
Hot Raspberry Delight, The Ott House 156
Irish Coffee, Middleton Tavern 56
Leo's Kiss, Milton Inn 120
Melon Colada, Kate Bunting's 7
Peppermint Cocoa, The Ott House 156
Wassail Punch, Milton Inn 119

BREADS
Applesauce Nut Bread, The Casselman 184
Cranberry Muffins, Robert Morris Inn 23
Orange Bread, Kitty Knight House 40
Pancakes, The Pasadena 28
Popovers, Normandie Farm 83
Pumpkin Bread, The Chimney Corner 200
Raised Buckwheat Cakes, The Chimney Corner 200
Southern Spoonbread, Commander Hotel 4
Yeast Rolls, Harrison's Chesapeake House 35

DESSERTS
Cakes:
Amaretto Cheesecake, The Penwick House 68
Apple Dapple Cake, Old South Mountain Inn 159
Chocolate Sabayon Cake, Brass Elephant 91
Coffee Cake, Society Hill 107
Mocha Nut Torte, The Province 147
Peach Brandy Pound Cake, Commander Hotel 4

Miscellaneous:
Apple Strudel, Fred Warner's 175
Bread Pudding in Lemon Rum Sauce, The Manor Tavern 124
Chocolate Mousse, Old Angler's Inn 88
Coconut Lust, Fran O'Brien's 43
Cornish Pudding, Cornish Manor 191
Croissant-Peanut Melt, Blair Mansion Inn 72
Damson Preserves, The Pasadena 28
Fig Preserves, The Pasadena 27
Rice Custard, Hotel Inn 15
Strawberry Sorbet, Country Fare Inn 111

Pies:
Blueberry Cassis Pie, Cozy Restaurant 152
Bob Andy Pie, Penn Alps 188
Macaroon Pie, Mrs. K's Toll House 75
Peach Pie, Cockey's Tavern 127
Pecan Pie, Mealey's 135
Shoofly Pie, The Casselman 184
Slice Lemon Pie, Mrs. K's Toll House 75
Strawberry Pie, Haussner's 99

Crusts:
Apple Strudel Pastry Dough, Fred Warner's 175
Blueberry Cassis Pie Meringue Crust, Cozy Restaurant 152
Coconut Lust Crust, Fran O'Brien's 43
Peach Pie Crust, Cockey's Tavern 127
Slice Lemon Pie Pastry Crust, Mrs. K's Toll House 75

ENTREES
Fowl:
Blackstone's Special (Chicken Tarragon), Brook Farm Inn of Magic 80
Chicken Champagne, Maggie's 132
Chicken Livers with Mushrooms and Tomatoes, Maggie's 131
Coq au Vin, Au Petit Paris 179
Le Canard Roti au Poivre Vert, Country Fare Inn 111
Parisian Poulet, The Province 148
Pollo Alla Romana, L'Osteria 172
Rum Raisin Duck, The Chambers 19
Sautéed Chicken Breast, Bushwaller's 139

Meats:
Beef and Mushrooms Andrea, Bistro 168

Beef and Scallops Sauté, Bushwaller's 140
Calves Liver with Wine Sauce, Bistro 168
Crisfield Steak, Chesapeake Restaurant 96
Filet de Boeuf Wellington, Normandie Farm 84
Frog Legs Forestière, PC's 195
Italian Hot Pot, Society Hill 107
Lamb Bandit Style, Manayunk Tavern 143
My Lady's Choice (Veal), The Manor Tavern 123
Roti de Porc, Au Petit Paris 180
Sauerbraten, Haussner's 100
Stuffed Pork Chops, Kate Bunting's 8
Veal Boloxi, The Inn at Perry Cabin 32
Veal Francese à la Sabatino, Sabatino's 103
Veal Maria, L'Osteria 171
Veal Normande, Cockey's Tavern 128
Veal Oskar, The Treaty of Paris 64

Miscellaneous:
Fettuccine Primavera, Fiori 115
Spaghetti and Marinara Sauce, Sabatino's 104

Seafood:
Bay Scallops Sienna, L'Osteria 171
Beef and Scallops Sauté, Bushwaller's 140
Broiled Backfin Crabmeat, Captain's Galley 11
Broiled Sea Trout, Harrison's Chesapeake House 36
Butterfly Shrimp Stuffed with Crab Imperial, The Chambers 20
Clams Casino, Cockey's Tavern 128
Crab à la Maryland, Cornish Manor 192

202

Crab Balls, The Chambers 19

Crab Cakes, Harrison's Chesapeake House 36

Crab Imperial, Blair Mansion Inn 71

Crab Imperial, The Inn at Perry Cabin 31

Crab Imperial, The Pasadena 27

Crabmeat Salad, Captain's Galley 12

Fried Count Oyster Sandwich, Dutch Kitchen 164

Lobster Luicci, Middleton Tavern 56

Maryland Bar-B-Que Shrimp, Riordan's 60

Oysters à la Gino, Robert Morris Inn 24

Oysters Baltimore, Chesapeake Restaurant 95

Oysters Browne, Harry Browne's 48

Oysters Coleman, Kate Bunting's 8

Oyster Corn Chowder, McGarvey's 52

Oysters Roberto, The Ott House 155

Scallop Casserole, Robert Morris Inn 23

Seafood Imperial, Hotel Inn 16

Seafood Mornay Randell, Riordan's 59

Seafood Stuffing, Fran O'Brien's 44

Sea Scallops with Morels and Cream Sauce, Old Angler's Inn 87

Shrimp and Scallops Marinara, Brass Elephant 92

Shrimp Creole, PC's 196

Shrimp James, McGarvey's 52

Shrimp Sautéed with Garlic Butter, Old Angler's Inn 88

Shrimp Scampi, Sabatino's 104

Spicy One (Red Snapper), Captain's Galley 12

Soft-Shelled Crabs, Old South Mountain Inn 160

SALADS

Annapolitan Salad, The Treaty of Paris 63

Captain Jack's Carrot Salad, Commander Hotel 3

Coleslaw, Mealey's 136

Crabmeat Salad, Captain's Galley 12

"Eleanora" Salad, Milton Inn 120

Hot Spinach Salad, Chesapeake Restaurant 95

Spaghetti Salad, The Chimney Corner 199

SANDWICHES

Annapolitan Sandwich, McGarvey's 52

California Connection, Society Hill 108

Country Ham Sandwich, Dutch Kitchen 164

Jay Schwartz, Harry Browne's 47

Old Fashioned Club Sandwich, Mealey's 136

R. B. Taney's Sandwich, Bushwaller's 139

Welch Rarebit, Harry Browne's 48

SAUCES, GRAVIES AND DRESSINGS

Andrea Sauce, Bistro 168

Blue Cheese Dressing, Dutch Kitchen 163

Casino Butter, Cockey's Tavern 128

Chicken Stuffing, Penn Alps 188

Chicken Tarragon Sauce, Brook Farm Inn of Magic 80

"Eleanora" Salad Dressing, Milton Inn 120

Green Goddess Dressing, The Treaty of Paris 63

203

Hansel Mountain Mamma Dressing, Fred Warner's 176
Jus Lie (Brown Sauce substitute), Maggie's 132
Lemon Rum Sauce, The Manor Tavern 124
Marinara Sauce, Fiori 115
Marinara Sauce, Sabatino's 104
Maryland Bar-B-Que Shrimp Sauce, Riordan's 60
Mornay Sauce, The Manor Tavern 123
Mustard Sauce, Fran O'Brien's 44
Vinaigrette Dressing, Chesapeake Restaurant 96

SOUPS

Bean Soup, The Chimney Corner 199
Bean Soup with Country Ham, Dutch Kitchen 164
Chili, The Ott House 156
Corn Soup, Cozy Restaurant 151
Crab, Asparagus and Cheddar Cheese Soup, McGarvey's 51
Crab Bisque, Kitty Knight House 39
Cuban Black Bean Soup, Middleton Tavern 55
Onion Soup Bistro, Bistro 167
Oyster Corn Chowder, McGarvey's 52
Portuguese Kale Soup, Brook Farm Inn of Magic 79
Tomato Soup, Old South Mountain Inn 160

VEGETABLES

Asparagus in Fillo, Manayunk Tavern 144
Baked Beans, The Casselman 183
Brad's Choice Zucchini Casserole, Riordan's 59
Brussel Sprouts Dijonnaise, Maggie's 131
Brussel Sprouts in Fennel, Manayunk Tavern 144
Dried Corn, Penn Alps 187
French-Fried Vegetables, Kitty Knight House 40
Green Beans, Normandie Farm 83
Sauerkraut, Fred Warner's 176
Sherried Acorn Squash, Mrs. K's Toll House 76
Spinach Pie, Fiori 116
Stewed Tomatoes, Hotel Inn 16
Stuffed Baked Potatoes, Fran O'Brien's 44